Ascended Masters of Color - Ascended Beings of Light

The Origin and Mission of People of Color

by
Grandmaster Anakhanda Mushaba

Edited by: Caroline Hazelton

This book is a work of non-fiction. Unless otherwise noted, the author and the publisher make no explicit guarantees as to the accuracy of the information contained in this book and in some cases, names of people and places have been altered to protect their privacy.

© 2005 Grandmaster Anakhanda Mushaba. All Rights Reserved.

No part of this book may be reproduced, stored in a retrieval system, or transmitted by any means without the written permission of the author.

First published by 1stBooks 10/25/05

ISBN: 1-4107-1464-0 (sc)

Printed in the United States of America
Bloomington, Indiana

This book is printed on acid-free paper.

Table of Contents

About The Author ix

Acknowledgements xi

Foreword xiii

Introduction xvii

Chapter 1 The Black Peoples Mission 1

Chapter 2 Historical Figures Of The Black Race 22

Chapter 3 The Black Race Origin And Other Historical Figures 33

Chapter 4 Psychological damage and its effects 64

Chapter 5 The Great Divine Experiment 78

Chapter 6 Ascended Master Afra Speaks 100

Chapter 7 A Word From Archangel Michael 113

Chapter 8 A Talk With The Master 116

Chapter 9 Questions And Answers 129

Chapter 10 I Am Your Brother - I Am Your Sister 138

Chapter 11 Africa Needs Change 144

Chapter 12 PASSING THE MANTLE OF KNOWLEDGE 148

Chapter 13 The Detriment of Religion To The Black Race..........................158

Chapter 14 Gurhan from Andromeda and the Galactic Council....................164

Chapter 15 An Entity Called Nigger......................169

Chapter 16 The First And The Seventh Ray Energy..............................177

Chapter 17 Djwhal Khul's Message To Anakhanda 180

Chapter 18 Adama-High Priest of Telos under Mt. Shasta 204

Chapter 19 Ascended Master Afra Returns............209

Chapter 20 The reconnections bring forth a message 211

Chapter 21 A Closing Message 215

Appendix....................................220

GRANDMASTER ANAKHANDA

About The Author

Anakhanda Mushaba became conscious of his connection with spirit around the age of 5 years old. At this age he used to lie in his bed and look upon his ceiling as if it were a motion picture screen as pictures would scroll across his ceiling along with a voice speaking in a language that was not of this earth. There was a hand that was writing and a voice speaking and interpreting what was being written. Even though he was not conscious of what was being written and spoken; he later found out that it was himself writing the script for his life. The language was from his home planet located in the Pleiades star system called Planet Mushaba. He has been watched over and nurtured personally by the Goddess Sophia, herself, because of what he has come to do on earth part of this according to the Council, is to be one of the world teachers servicing humanity.

Anakhanda Mushaba whose race originated in the Andromeda Galaxy, the home of very highly evolved beings, incarnated on Earth to serve humanity during the time of great change and ascension. He is the chief representative on Earth for the Mushaba Force- Mushaba Light which is a very amazing and powerful Creation Force, Life Force, a force that unifies, transforms and gives one Freedom and Empowerment. He is what you call an Original Master of the Mushaba Force. He is responsible for the Mushaba Force being brought forward into being from what is called the Original Force. He was given approval by the Council of Creation, who must approve all new creations, to bring this Mushaba

Force to the third dimensional planet Earth and to use it to help evolve humanity, among many other things.

The Mushaba Force carries the original codes and energy used in the evolution of Earths humanity which propelled humanity forward approximately 373 thousand years and was used to initiate the so called "big bang" that created our present universe. His name Mushaba is taken from the force and the race that he represents, the force is not named after him.

Ana: means **light** and khanda: means **the pathway to knowledge**. Mushaba means **Freedom and Empowerment** and **Divine Love and Oneness** so his name means, "One who lights the pathway to knowledge with divine love and oneness.' It also means the "Mother Force" and **"He who leads the people to freedom"**. He is a teacher of Universal White Time Healing and a level 4 practitioner, a New Earth Teacher and a Reiki Master and Teacher. He is an author that has not only released this book which addresses those beautiful beings of color that is very much unknown to humanity; But he has several books that will soon be available which you could find more about in the appendix. He is a lecturer, teacher, and channel and offers workshops in various trainings and is also involved in alternative healing and fitness and provides many services using the awesome power of The Mushaba Force.

Acknowledgements

I would like to give acknowledgement to all of spirit which includes the Archangels, the Angelic kingdom, the Ascended Masters, my own Master Self Within and the Source of All Energies. I would like to thank those who assisted me with information through their services of channeling various entities to bring forward information, to those from the inner realms who brought information to me through the various means of telepathy and intuition. I want to say that I am ever so grateful and very, very appreciative to spirit for all the help and guidance given to me since my physical birth in this earth realm. It has been one fantastic adventure of life which includes all the elements of an adventure; hardships, journeys, good times, bad times, joys, sadness, discoveries, mystical happenings, and dangers. I am happy to be a part of the divine timing and plan for the greater good of creation.

I have to, as always; thank my parents Wali and Min'Imah for their powerful foundation of support in more ways than I could ever say. They are my greatest inspiration and love, Aleem and Paravun I thank them for their dedication and support to all that we do as Mushaba Spiritual Warriors, Masters and Commanders of the Force and for the great wisdoms they display and share with me always. They are two very special and unique vibrations of spirit force. I like to thank my spiritual son Karriem for the motivation and support he gives simply by the life and thoughts that he share, with me so profoundly. His connection with spirit has always been pure. To those who I have not mentioned, know that you are a part of this circle of expression and gratitude and you know who you are.

Foreword

I ask that the reader have a very open mind, especially if you are one who seeks the truth. What will be presented here may be different from what you have read in the past. This information is from an esoteric spiritual source and point of awareness, which may not agree with the usual sources of information brought forward concerning this subject. This book is about ascended masters and ascended beings of light. It revolves around not only those ascended master of various races we usually hear about, but it also revolves around the ascended masters of color, namely Black or African ascended beings. In using the description "African people," I am referring to what is termed the Black race. I want it to be clear and understood that the mention of African People does not in any way limit them to people on the African continent. African people are referring to the origin of the black race which started in Africa. We are speaking of the black or dark skinned people in general whether they are called Africans or African American.

What we are attempting to do here is bridge the misunderstanding concerning the race issue. We ask that you read the book and a greater clarity will be given about all of this and a brighter light of understanding will be brought forward concerning African/Black origins. There are unfortunately, so many misperceptions about Africans and Blacks both as words and as a people. Some people find it racist to say Black race and to others it is a turn off. Some find African not to be inclusive of Black people in general but only of the people on the African continent. What is important here is that people of all colors, nationalities and cultures read the information contained within these pages. The information is incredible and mind expanding and we need to put all the judgments aside and read without prejudgment of the contents. It is really sad that there are so many judgments and misunderstandings among people that one has to go through a long drawn out explanation in an attempt to explain the point and to avoid prejudgment.

This is the information as brought forward to humanity by those masterful beings and archangels within the spiritual realms of light. Even though Earth's history has been so tampered with and so much misinformation has been brought forward that, for the most part, people accept what is given or written as true history. Believe me, history is seriously warped and this book is an attempt to help straighten some of this out. We have been given so many versions of history, of his-story and we go around speaking this misunderstanding and we are only repeating what has been written. This book brings another look at history and the truth surrounding humanity, the coming of the African people, and their mission. This is a must read! I am really tired of all these semantics as to how one should say this or that or use this word instead of that word. None of this really matters if it is all basically lies anyway, now does it? None of this matter if people are still going to be continuously separated and be full of hate because of perceived differences now does it? We present another perspective to at least consider and search within our own selves for that which we feel is true. Because, when you see all this from a higher galactic perspective, a higher spiritual perspective it is all very different. So please, as you read this book I ask you not to get caught up or lost in what name a people should be called, whether its White, Black, Caucasian, African, Red, Yellow, or Brown. Get the knowledge of what is being presented and have an open mind and most importantly, have an open heart. It is amazing how people can become turned off by the use of certain words, and even feels insulted. This shuts us down from being open to what is truly being said. We are not trying to be scholarly I just want all people to read and understand, for this is what is important. We must wake up as a humanity and look at depth of things. It would really be a great injustice and not serve the light and the truth if people of various races take this information as only for a certain group of people.

This is universal information that is about all people. People live in too much fear and misunderstanding about each other, as individuals and as a race. We as spiritual beings seeking the truth must be open to the knowledge that is coming forward from the higher realms. Almost 100% of what we are taught on earth is untruth and manipulation for purpose of control. I went through much agonizing over the correct title for this book, so not to offend any particular race of people and also not to present it as a "Black book." Spirit and I went back and forth until we found what we felt would be an appropriate title and would actually capture the interest of people of all races. People, regardless of color, who say they are spiritual, and frown upon any race are not spiritual nor as deep as they think they are. They need to look seriously in the mirror, and look back at themselves because that is the only place the problem lies. Every race had, has and will have their great contribution to humanity, which is how it should be. This is what makes a human

family a oneness; all people working and contributing to the upliftment of humanity and the greater plan of the source of creation.
Anakhanda Shaka Mushaba

Introduction

I would first like to say that even though this book has been revised for the sake of clarity, the content remains true to the original version.

The information contained within this very powerful and provocative book, will open up an entire new era of universal understanding. It will help to explain the mission of the people of color and why they are under going their past and present and conditions. I warn you, this is information has not been available before now. It has been blocked or hidden from the consciousness of all races of people, for a greater reason than has been known before now. It needed to be a certain and specific time reached before this information could come forward. It had to be brought forward in a new movement of uncovering the hidden truths and the revealing of the unknown. The issue of race has always been very sensitive. It is something that not only the white race has not been open to, but also the black race. And also understand that people and mediums of a spiritual nature were not open to receiving this information. They never entertained the thought that it was possible, that there is such a thing as Black Race Ascended beings.

I will attempt to bring clarity to this issue once and for all. The reader is asked to keep a clear and open mind in order to be able to accept the knowledge and wisdom that you are about to receive from the reading of this book. I'm telling you, what you are about to read will be to some, shocking, controversial and will basically blow the lid of misunderstanding off of your mind and unawareness. It will tell of things that some will not want to believe and some will feel strongly and know within that it is the truth and they will resonate with this truth. It will help to change the understanding of people all over the world about what the real truth is concerning this entire black race issue and will send shock waves across the planet. It is not to point a finger at anyone or any race. It is not brought forward to prove any one right or wrong. It is simply the truth that should be known. This will cause a great leap in growth for those who can understand and accept what is written here. It has been uncovered finally, by the Mushaba Force. It is part of the Mushaba Force's mission to bring this forward to all humanity. It is truly amazing to say the least. If you are ready, let us begin the sharing of the story.

CHAPTER 1
<u>The Black Peoples Mission</u>

When did this whole affair start concerning the Black race? It goes back beyond the knowledge that has been available to this world. It goes back to the first universe were information concerning it is no longer available. The name of the first universe is spelled Prohibitivus but the pronunciation eludes the human vocabulary. This connection includes the Blue and Violet races as well. It goes back before the planet of Sirius which is located in this present known universe. Prohibitivus was one of the original twelve universes of so long ago it is beyond human comprehension. It is a rare few who still carry an aspect or connection with and from the 1st universe. Let me talk a little bit about the 1st universe before I begin the story of the seeding of the Black Race from the Planet Sirius. I will share with you information from the spiritual realms that was taken from the universal records, or the akashic records, which is the history of all things recorded in vibration. As I said, this information was not available before now because it has been blocked from the awareness of humanity for a very, very long time. However, now the time has come to make this information available to all humanity.

We at Mushaba Force have always wondered deeply and searched deeply for the understanding of why things are like they are concerning the Black race. We had so many questions and there was not a book on the planet that we were able to find that had the answers. We questioned spirit for many years without satisfaction. We were not given nor were we open to receive certain information until the time was right according to the timing of the Divine Plan. It is not about those of us in Mushaba Force who wanted to know the real truth. It was a much broader picture that at that moment we were not able to comprehend. It has a divine reasoning that was to be rectified in time. Finally, we were able to open up the contacts and information through spirit to access this information. We had no idea what was in store for but we knew it would be profound. Our minds and awareness were expanded beyond belief. We knew we would be privileged to gain access to this information because we were coming from the heart-seeking and not the mind-seeking. We were about the truth not about gaining information to cause more separation. It is a very sensitive subject, but it is a necessity that the truth be told, for the sake of a broader spiritual unity and oneness among all humanity.

Council of light

To begin with, let us share some information with you from the Council of Light. I asked the question, "Did Black People come from Sirius to this planet?"

The answer was: "Well, not exactly. It feels like there was a precursor to that. That, that wasn't the origin but it does feel like in a sense if you think about it in time that the connection with Sirius was way later, but the Black race was first and that's what the underlying jealousy is about, the Caucasian jealousy. That which came from the dark was the light and that it came back into the dark but it did not annihilate it. And because of that, it is trying to annihilate the dark so that it's first in lineage. But There's a place and it's spelled something like" Prohibitivus" and that place is where the seed of the Black race originated, but it was so far before Sirius. You know there are 12 universes and it was at the 1st universe where the Black seed came from. It wasn't in this current universe which is where Sirius is located. It was way before this universe so it has probably not been discovered or not acknowledged nor understood yet, but it will be before your life is over on this plane." According to the above statement the seed of the Black race goes back way beyond the knowledge of what is known by humanity. It opens up much speculation and research needs to be conducted on finding out information that pertains to the 1st universe. This is very difficult since knowledge of it is unavailable. This will take research from spiritual sources that have access to this information. I will continue until the information is uncovered for humanity.

Another question asked the Council of Light was: "What do you see concerning these issues surrounding Black people and this whole spiritual pathway"? The answer was as follows:

"Well, the most important thing to remember about the separation of spirit and form is that it has played itself out in different conditions and the different choices that have been made around those conditions. It's not about Black or White as much as it is about light and the absence of light. We see it as a racial process, the many colors, the red skin, olive skin, yellow skin and what ever skin. If you talk to a red skin person, you would probably get the same response as from a black skinned person or a yellow skinned person. So what's interesting is, is that it's all a projection of the inner separation from light. Everyone wants light, and therefore feels, that it is in some way, related to color, it's related to density, it's related to right and wrong. So the duality, is the separation of spirit and form, is really what is being worked through on all levels.

If one thinks about the duality, as we spoke to you about the battle, they're were those who wanted to do battle and those who wanted peace, being at odds with each other in most situations. This means that it is getting played out so that the battle can create peace. If you think about the same thing there are 2 sides, there is an inner and an outer, that's how it seems to us. Once there is a separation and thought forms are attached to that separation, then there are levels upon levels of challenges that are created in terms of individuals seeing each other clearly. Because so many things get wrapped up into ideals or models, or the roles or the ethnicity, or what ever it is, and the separation gets more and more extreme, more and deeper, and deeper and more uncomfortable for people. At the same time, it's not about what it seems to be about. So, one wants to exercise caution when talking about the separation and labeling it and trying to define things around it in terms of giving it meaning, this actually creates more of the separation because it becomes more entrenched in thought forms. It doesn't mean that the pain should be overlooked. It means that the literal reason that the separation exists is because of the free will experiment. So, if one wants to knock something, one should knock the free will experiment as you Anakhanda is doing and do the best to bring the union about, the oneness of all there is so that all of it disappears, not just part of it or just part of it is looked at and that's how we, the council feel about it. There are so many ironies, in the Black/White thing, for instance, White people going out trying to get dark for example, and so one of the things that are important is to laugh at it and at the same time you try to make a story about it. Make a story about it instead of giving it meaning. Teach people through the story how silly it is to in any way, look at things as if they are not the same; it is not o k. to do that."

Author's Comments:

What is basically being said here is that a choice was made to play something out for the betterment and growth of humanity, a role that the Black race accepted. Why did the Black race accept this role? Let's see what other spiritual masters have to say about this.

Sananda (Jesus)

Presented are questions that were asked Sananda (Jesus).

(Q). Why aren't Black people more prominently involved in the metaphysical-spiritual pursuits of knowledge and the developing of various abilities such as having alien contact, channeling, direct contact with angelic beings, and Ascended Masters?

(A). Interesting question! I would say that sometime when a group of beings have to concentrate, because of circumstances and the acquisition of physical comforts and equality in a physical way and in an emotional way and so forth, that the spiritual element, which is almost a luxury for that group, is put off in a certain way or discarded or actually rejected because of the pain and the burden of really making everything else come together in their physical, material life. They have taken on an element of suffering for the planet and they are not lesser for that, but in many cases greater beings, with more quality within the soul and can basically shoulder this sort of burden and this sort of choice much easier than their other brothers and sisters of different races on the earth, and therefore, have taken on this responsibility. And they have found themselves evolving through families and situations and in countries where they really didn't have the comforts or the luxuries to explore certain things. They're still their, they're still divine, they're totally divine and almost there is what I would call a certain degree of poverty or difficulty that exist in the African continent itself, difficulties in climates, difficulties in circumstances in everyday life, so that there might not be that feeling of luxury or necessity to step up to the new age ladder. There is also getting caught in the crux of feeling disappointed, hurt and maybe going in the opposite direction and saying "who can I trust?" You might say, what about India? They are in a lot of poverty as a people and a lot of difficulty as a people and yet, it seems that the country itself has a lot of spiritual quality whether it is conceptual or whether it is true, there are a lot of ways to look at it because they focus primarily on the spiritual, with a long spiritual leg and a short physical leg. So basically, were saying, because of circumstances in your country of America, because of the whole slavery syndrome, there has been almost a downward spiral and a loss of hope, it has been a very difficult cost for the Black race. Because of that, there has been a reluctance in some ways to look to things beyond the earth. Now, there are many different religions and many different practices that you know of that people look to on Earth but not beyond Earth.

The influence of the White Race

Almost the whole ascended community, and that whole sense of what is termed the Ascended Master Consciousness has been explored in the same way. One of the reasons is because of the influence of the White race which is basically to cloud out and cover up with their own concepts and misinformation, to cloud out the inclusion, within the community of Ascended Masters, the whole idea of a Black Madonna. They would paint them all with White faces. All of this is to make one think that this isn't for me and so I'm not going there. And then, covered with that is the difficulty within society to achieve a certain degree of equality and physicality of comfort and all of that. So there's been more of a reluctance to go there and almost this feeling of "who really am I?"

The true roots

There is the problem of being so severed from their true roots, their true awareness of where they come from, their true reality and yet, many of the Black race came from Sirius and from very evolved star systems. They came with the idea of bringing higher consciousness and, actually, you might almost say, they have certain abilities that aren't seen. This is because of the Sirian aspect, the Sirian blood that runs in many of the beings with the darker skin. They have abilities of strength and wisdom. For the Black race on earth, it's almost like being on a different planet than everyone else, also interesting! And because of this, there is this inherent feeling among the White community that these people are different from us and they (the Black race), always saying: "Well no! We are the same, were all the same." But actually, there is a difference and the differences are quite wondrous! The differences are just a part of the diversity of the planet.

There are certain illnesses that the Black race is more susceptible to than the White race. It's because of a different strain of blood. Now, all of this has been mixed and intermixed so much that it isn't as obvious as it once was. We could say that the manipulations that are going on, on the Earth, have taken a little bit of the open heartedness out, but it never dies.

Author's Comments:

There is a Black Race of Beings called the Mushaba Race that has a very important and interesting history. This Race has a direct impact and a great significance to the history of humanity and it's evolvement. It was this Race that made possible, through it's genetic codes, the appearance of what we know as the human being. This subject will be discussed at length in upcoming books.

Demonstrating the heart

The Black race more than any other race on the planet Earth has a great capacity to fully demonstrate heart, and demonstrates the love of the heart and the truth of the heart and the soul more than any other race. It's almost as if they can take more because the heart can and they can give more. They are almost willing to take more and carry and shoulder more than the others and they are not less spiritual for this. It isn't that at all. In fact, as soon as they get up "in the airplane" that Metatron spoke of, they will have it all. But their difficulty on the earth and what has happened here has really taken a large toll. They (the Black race) really had really large crosses to carry in some ways, but they will be rewarded.

*Note: The airplane spoken of is the reference Archangel Metatron made concerning seeing things from a higher, wider perspective, as if going up in an airplane, which allows one to see further and see more, from a higher perspective.

My next questions was based on what I felt within myself and wanted to hear what spirit had to say to see if it coincided with my inner feelings, which it did. This question was asked of Sananda:

(Q). Why did I choose Black skin this time?

(A) Actually as an equalizer. You had black skin before, and you have had other skins before as an equalizer to put your force, your magnitude, and your weight on that side of the coin, because there are sides taken on the earth. But actually to want to bring it together, there is part of you that would like to unite all the religions, not only all of the races. It is for unity and in order to broadcast unity within diversity, and oneness within duality and polarity, you chose to do it from the harder position, from one sense. It is a wake up call and a demonstration that says "here, let me give back some hope, let me demonstrate that were actually part of all of those races and that all races are the same.

There is some unifying thread in all religions, and all races, and all of it. And that is that we are all from Source. So you will bring that, you are already doing that. Some how this broadcasting the signal goes further with the Black skin as you call it, because there are many that will hear you that haven't listened to anyone else. They can hear you, you have the heart, you have the soul, and you understand the earth and you understand the heavens. You understand the cause, you can put yourself in their shoes and you will speak for them as a leader. So how interesting!"

The uniting of all people

I do not like to see this division at all and I would like to see the point at which the churches would unite and all of the tribes would unite and all of the groupings would unite and everything comes into a sharing, where there is a forgiveness for the ignorance that has been on the earth, and that everyone begins to see that they're all together in this, that they are all in a humanitarian sort of energy that is very, very uniquely diverse. As Metatron said, "very unique." Most planets do not have more than one or two or maybe three races, certainly not the abundant diversity of humans, and they also are not pitted against each other. They're in unity and they do not even see the differences, most of them. So it is very interesting to be able to come to terms in peace and understanding that the heart has no color and to go beyond the boundaries of the skin and the physical form and temple. And altogether it is going to supply as Metatron said, the universe, the galaxy and everyone else reading these books that are now being written with a magnificent sort of victory.

Because the play that was played out and the parts that were given were very difficult ones, and I would say, that perhaps the Black race took the hardest parts in some ways, but then they were up to it. So there is no color in truth, only on earth. And there are no physical bodies in some ways, it's all temporary so the parts are temporary. So you chose a Black body because you were in alignment, because you have the sensitivity. Perhaps, because that is the race you might have seen that, in some way, is the underdog on the Earth. They received the most punishment, the most difficulties in some ways, and the most judgments in some ways and have the least power, world power. But they have heart power. This is not the least, it is possibly the most."

Author's comments:

So what is being said here is simply that the Black race has come here on a great mission to teach humanity what can happen when one is divided through separation and looking more to the outer than to the inner. Think about it for a moment. The Black race has been put through some of the most unbelievable suffering that one can imagine and has suffered losses as high as, from some estimates, approx. 100 million plus people. And yet, the Black race is still so full of love and forgiveness. With all the deadly treatment given to Black people, they still turn right around and stick out their hand to offer help to anyone, whatever color they may be. What is this saying about the heart of Black people? What is this saying about being able to take more and accept more? This was a very, very difficult and nearly impossible mission that was accepted. There were those of the Black skin who were here and decided to leave because they did not want to continue with this experiment, this mission. It was too hard for some but some remained just the same.

Look also at how this whole scenario played out from slavery to, the white washing of all the great figures in history, such as Jesus Moses, Isis, and many others who are all portrayed as White skinned people. This will be addressed in later chapters. I questioned the Masters about why no one had heard of or channeled an African race Ascended Master. It is unheard of on the spiritual pathway, to say the least. This goes back even before slavery when the dark skinned people were at odds with each other. They were in separation before slavery. They were warring among themselves due to perceived differences. It was a great responsibility for the dark skinned people to shoulder yet, someone had to have the heart to fulfill this mission, this free will experiment. It is a free will experiment and no one is forced to accept it. The Black race agreed to accept this role. All this was for the bigger, broader picture for humanity that was to be played out. This information has been withheld or blocked for a very, very long time. But to coincide with what was said; let us hear from Ascended Master Djwhal Khul known also as D.K

D.K.

As you, the reader, continue to follow my line of questioning, you will see that I have no problem in being very direct with spirit.

(Q). Why aren't Black people participating more fully in this whole spiritual movement with more direct involvement, and are there any Black Ascended Masters. There is a great imbalance in this area and why haven't anything been done by the Spiritual Hierarchy to rectify this problem?

(A). Interesting! Well, the Black people as you say on this planet, they were seeded from many worlds, They didn't come from this world, They came from higher worlds and have a larger perspective and a massive heart.

I would say, in order to take on the mission that they did take on, they had to have massive heart. And remember they were not the only ones seeded, the yellow race and others also were also seeded. And I need to share with you, that in the creation and in the bringing of the beings, all the different races, to earth, something was to be played out, in diversity and oneness, and the link between diversity and oneness. But I also need to share with you, that in Africa, where many of the Black races were first introduced to the planet, certain attunements happened, and I don't look at them as being good or bad. I simply look at them as choices made to uplift the whole, like Jesus made.

When Jesus came, he seeded certain things into the grid of the earth. He had to go through certain experiences to reveal it to others. In some ways, the Black race has chosen, because of its heart, to emphasize the need, the absolute need to look within for truth and not look without. However, because when something needs to be demonstrated, it needs to be played out. You can't just talk about things you need to see them. It is a world of form; it is a world of visuality. Therefore, if you look, back and you look at the races, the Black race living in Africa, you will see, even before the White colonization and the European contract came in, that there was a certain alliance with much, much higher beings. They're high beings in the African arts and in the African legends. You will see pictures of ships and connections with off-worlders in the African legends. You will see pictures of ships and connections with off-worlders in the African Arts. It is there, and the Ancients were very highly developed spiritually, and so that was there.

Different attunements among the people

However, something was played out, and it was a bit of a choice to play it out. It was almost like a crossroads to play out. What I'm talking about is that the people did have attunements to others, to other ideas. But even amongst themselves, even before the Whites, the European contracts came and brought attunements that were disappointing and obviously controlling, very controlling, and created more and more divisions, there were already divisions among the African people living in Africa. These divisions assembled into tribes which had different lifestyles, different cultures, and lived in different ways. These divisions were made according to the color of the skin, Interesting! So the same thing is being played out in some ways in other parts of the world, but it began even there in Africa. And you would say, "Why is that?" "Why would the Black race divide itself by the color of its skin?" What was being played out? When you go to a higher perspective and look at it, is simply this; They were seeded, They came from other worlds and planets, and they weren't all the same. They came from many worlds and they were in contact in Africa that is the Ancient ones, with off-worlders constantly. They had intergalactic contact all the time. They had many new ideas, many influences that came in and some imbalance did enter, obviously, because of the divisions that happened.

And so what happened, is they begun to play out and demonstrate for the world what happens when you look more outer, rather than inner. They had daily contact with certain of those who were considered Gods, because they came from the sky, and they had different wisdoms. They divided into factions very quickly. Interesting why they divided into factions so quickly and why it was by skin color that they divided. The skin color itself became a divisive force amongst the people. What happened was that there was a certain translation of truth that got little imbalances in it, a lack of attunement in it somewhere, because truth is unity not separation. Somehow, in our experience and how we see it, is that they chose, although it is not remembered, and it is not consciously known.

The Ancients that we spoke of, who were in contact with off worlders, were in certain tribes. The Aborigine tribes are very, very ancient and they hold and held and maintained much of their knowledge, their more secret knowledge. Some of the tribes in Africa got a little bit what you would call out of attunement, some left and some of the knowledge became a little bit lost, a little bit extinct. This is not a fault, it doesn't mean that they did something wrong, it's just part of the process. Before the White race came, yes, there were separations amongst the tribes and certain truths got lost. Please understand that it is not always the fault of the people. Like I said before, imbalances came into the Earth from losing its moon, from disturbance in the atmosphere, from catastrophes within the Solar System causing some to leave, some to shift, and some to forget causing many repercussions. Things may have gone a little bit farther than originally intended. I would say that this is true. Imbalance causes more imbalance. Think of it like an airplane slightly off course. If it continues, all of a sudden, by the end of the day, it is very much off course. So things simply happen.

A choice to teach:

They chose to actually demonstrate what happens when you look outward rather than inward. What does that mean? It means that they had to somehow live with diversity and somehow, through polarity and dualism and diversity move to oneness and life, and bring everything into a higher point. So they had deep spirituality, they retain it still. Could they maintain it when they chose to reveal what happens in divisions? So you know they had intergalactic contact and you know the Ancients in Africa had this and were in communion and it was reflected in art and in legend, all the flying machines and so forth which depicted the space ships. They had deep soul and heart connections. It is only the mind that interprets love, not the soul and the heart.

When the European contact came, the people were already in a certain amount of division, not because they were bad or evil, but because they were allowing themselves to portray this sort of looking outward, making divisions based on something external rather than internal, not finding what was the soul, but finding out what were the differences. Some of this is because of genetic imprinting. So it doesn't go to the fault of the people at all. The Chinese do it. Every race on earth has genetic imprinting of where they originally came from which was a planet of just that people. They came to a planet with all of it and they maintained a certain amount of genetic imprinting of differences. It isn't a bad thing, it isn't a good thing, its just is. The knowledge, the idea, the mission was to bring all of this together and then, have it all come into unity in spite of genetic imprinting which was actually a very powerful thing.

Division among the people

What happened when the Europeans came to Africa, was that the situation that was already in division became more damaging. The people were already in a certain amount of conflict because of differences. They were living in different ways and had different cultures already. Then here comes another group of people creating more division. This is not totally out of or missing in genetic memory. Often times a group comes from out of the sky. E.T's has come, and they landed in a new world, and they were considered Gods. They had a negative mission, to take over, to control, and because they seem to just have come here from the skies, they were considered superior, or the people thought they were superior. They (E.T's), acted as if they were and the people had forgotten about the flying machines or craft so they looked up to those from the craft. The European contact and the force that they came with were misconstrued and more division was created.

So what happens is that when a group of people still hold it in their memories, the different seeds of all the different races that they had at that time, the fact is that they make some divisions of their own based on something external. What happens is, is that they lose a little bit of their link to spirit when they start looking outside so much. Every race has done it. The White race certainly has done it. They lost their sensitivity to truth, lost their link to spirit to a degree. But what happened is that the White race maintained that economic stranglehold that they had. What happened with some of the Black races is that they lost a little bit of their deeper spirituality and their essences within because of the struggle, and because contact with the off worlders stopped happening. They look too much to the outer, and they are not keeping that link with spirit. It doesn't mean that something was wrong with the people. The circumstances were dictating this.

If you go back further, you will see that it was the choice to demonstrate it, reveal it, bring it up and heal it, and clear it. So basically, out of imbalance comes balance. But because this is forgotten and because of the lessening of the link with spirit, all of a sudden, that which is outer becomes more and more important, so that eventually all that there is, is the outer, and the link from within gets dimmer. Because of that, the circumstances snowball and so there it is. The lessons of poverty and the lessons of difficulties and struggle come in and then they take even more of the warped attention. So this division was already inherent in Africa, plus the White colonization, which was completely unnatural, and they even created unnatural boundaries that weren't even there. It created a world or land or people that were already in turmoil even before they were brought to America. So you are a people in some amount of turmoil. But not everyone is in turmoil. So they (the White race), brought them (the Black race), to another place and they brought with them what ever they had where ever they go.

Slave races and more division

Another factor is brought in by the slavery, creating a slave race. Now, the creation of slaves isn't something new. It happened in Atlantis and it is in the genetic memory. There have always been groups that have enslaved people. In Egypt, in Atlantis, they created slave races because of wanting to have domination and control. So it is a part of the turmoil that existed, with one thing leading to the next that lessened the spirituality to a degree. Then all the external factors come in that have to do with being distracted from spirit because of the difficulties. Somehow being kept more apathetic, more wanting to be even more divided into their separate groups because of the lack of love which then springs forth hatred from that to that, from one to another and everything sort of snowballs into something else. Did the whole Black nation lose its spirit? Of course not. What was the massive lesson? People need to see people as people.

So in south Africa, I would say to you that the hope there lies in leaders who will go beyond being Black or White. It doesn't matter if the leadership goes from one side to the other until a leader comes forth and goes beyond the external of being Black or White. That's where the hope lies. It's the looking within rather than the looking without. This was played out in Africa, and now its being played out in America by a group of people who have so much heart that they chose to play it out in America. I want you to know that it is not true that there is no Black Ascended Masters, and that none have ascended. What is true is that the veil, and the ignorance over the whole Earth because of White domination, has what you might say, stopped it up, created what is called a veil that covers or prevents certain information from coming in so that the channels do not have access to that information because it is blocked. Certain ones who brought in the early books were also living within that whole matrix of disunity; it's a very big story, a very long story.

What is the lesson? Accept change, accept the Universe. Somewhere the African tribes began to close down to Universal Consciousness and had to create a way to stay alive in their own divided factions, because they wanted to maintain their differences. I would say that this all played out, a sort of energy that needed to happen on the earth. The earth is a school and the Black Skinned Beings on the other worlds and the other planets are not playing this out there. It is only the ones who said, "I will go and I will play this out." So the Blacks were seeded from another world.

Taking the traces of origin back

Many of them mated with the ancients and many of the most spiritual and most evolved ones at one point in your history, decided to leave. What they said is "we will take all the traces with us," This is interesting is it not? They said "We are going to take all the traces with us, we're going to destroy our records and our knowledge, we're going to go back to those worlds from where we came, because this is too hard to do." Some left the earth because they said this was too difficult to demonstrate. Some of the seeded ones used their own power that they learned from the ancients and from the E. T's that came and lived with them, to dismantle what they have brought, so there were no traces. Then, certain natural destructions and wars also destroyed some knowledge, so empty spaces existed.

Bare in mind that at that time White beings from Europe came to Africa. Humanity usually didn't leave somewhere and go somewhere else unless something wasn't quite right and they were looking for a new place. When you are looking to move to a new place, it is because there is something you don't like about your current place.

Something is not right. Things are going not so well or badly or something. You don't usually look for change unless there is a need for it. There was a disintegration of their society and then they moved toward disintegrating another society. You can say, well this is negative. Well it is or it isn't. It's just is. But what has happened is that it illuminates the whole thing. Very, very big subject! It's not too big to be undone. It's addressed, it's known.

So please know that when a group demonstrates growth and struggle, it is not unlike the growth and struggle that was undertaken by the one called Jesus. He didn't demonstrate ease, he demonstrated struggle. It is always the higher path. It is not the lesser path. But for this path and this particular evolvement, bare in mind that free will choice at every moment also constantly brings in other preferences and motives so that the original intent of the ancients is changed as we go down the road. And so the little bit of struggle that was chosen to demonstrate something became massive struggle. If an airplane is off course 3 degrees that is not that much. But if it continues to stay the course, it gets to be way off. Then something has to be corrected so that it does not remain way off.

Author's Comments:

The above is saying a great deal and it leaves so much to be considered. The mission of the Black race is incredible and yet it was a free will choice. It did get off course a little bit and it continued in that direction taking it way off course. Things have to be set right to bring the balances back to the situation as originally intended.

Chapter 2
Historical Figures Of The Black Race

I would like to begin this chapter with a presentation of several questions that lead up to the information presented in this chapter. I want to know if this information about the origin of the Black race and the Black Race Ascended Masters would be unblocked and people would then be able to begin channeling these Black Race Ascended Masters and bring this information forward. I presented this question to Master D. K- Djwhal Khul.

(Q). Is there going to be a point at which this knowledge is going to be unblocked and people are going to be able to channel these Black Race Ascended Masters?

(A). "Absolutely! There are worlds and planets where all the people, the Beings are Black. There are also worlds where all the people are more of the yellow skin and the beliefs and the ways in which they live are very different than what has been played out on the earth. There are Masters in all of the worlds and it is not true that there is no Black Ascended Masters." I continued speaking with D.K. as to why I asked that question about the Black Race Ascended Masters. So I made the following statement:

"The fact that you don't talk to any, no one has channel any, and never heard of any makes you wonder if they exist."

(A). Well, let's just say that the White race is closed to it and let's say that the Black race is not open to it either, and so, for different reasons it has been veiled. And because of that inadequacy and that imbalance in the truth, there are many who say Mother Mary was Black, that Isis was Black and was there a Black Jesus, was Jesus Black? Jesus wasn't any color, and if he was that was not why he came and it isn't important. We almost like to devoid the use of colors because they bring in a certain amount of limitation to what was really happening. But there are many who know that there are Black Race Masters in the Heavens. They have Ascended, but the history is not there.

Author's Comment To D.K:

"This is the part I'm talking about and wanted to get clear on and that is, if a person has nothing but negativity to look up to, as has been depicted about the Black Race, it affects them mentally, psychologically, etc. I have never heard this issue of Black Race Masters addressed before."

Djwhal Khul

The way people have been controlled in your world is to get them not to think, not to have time to think. Thinking is what changes consciousness and it also changes genetics. The matrix has been White controlled but only by a few, a few Whites. They have controlled the entire corporate value system, flooding it with illusion and control. And a lot of this has almost, let's say, invisibly infiltrated spiritual channels and all beings everywhere without them even realizing it. That control is so deep and has gone on for so long that it is in the cellular memories and it is what needs to be repaired in cellular memory in all beings and divisions.

So a part of the Mushaba Force is to puncture a hole in disunity. How interesting to choose to do it in the midst of all of this. And that is why we said to you at one time that it needs to open up. The Mushaba Force needs to open up and go mainstream. It can't be a closed group, because it is because of closed groups, that it even came into being, the Mushaba Force, to open up these closed groups.

Some fear is held in the memory of Black people and rightfully so. Perhaps it could have been avoided. They have been dominated. They came with heart. They are heart people and they have allowed something to happen in order to take on a larger mission. Well it is tiresome. It's time we agree, we very much agree. And so all of that is being considered now. What we have talked about today amongst ourselves may sound like words but actually it has put a light on something that is rarely talked about. In fact, a book should be written about all of this but there is so much sensitivity in this area. There's a lot of sensitivity from every side and angle. So taking off these robes of sensitivity in all of that, because all the groups are clinging to their divisions at this time, because they feel that at least they have something that's supportive of them. It is from mistrust and lack of trust.

But your world is going to be changing. It is the three dimensional ideas that are still maintained and held onto with such a force, like one's life depends on it. These things are what prevent it from shifting out even faster. And so never underestimate the power of a group of three. Literally, do not underestimate what three can actually do. (this is in reference to the three of us who are working to bring this information to light). If they continue to teach and to think and to teach the young ones that they must be aware of the importance of keeping an internal connection to spirit, as number one.

Author:

I had thought about the spiritual hierarchy sending a Black Ascended Master to me to speak with me and for me to channel. So I ask the question to Master D.K.

(Q). Can the spiritual hierarchy contact a Black Race Ascended Master and have him come and speak with me, to channel with me, and to give telepathic information..

(A). It would be wonderful, what a wonderful idea! And so we will deliver this message. Don't think that it is you who block any of this. It is something in the collective humanity and it isn't you. So we can work with that and it is going to become evident soon.

There are many spiritual teachers out there on the Earth and again, from the White Race, I would say and because of all the things we have talked about, some of them are now putting themselves up as Gods. They are the last word, they are the incarnation of this and that and they have taken the pendulum a little to far. They don't need anyone, they are God incarnate. That is not accurate either. First your un-empowered, then you are in charge of everything and it isn't that either. It needs to be somewhere in the middle of balance.

Well you say, that not enough Black people are doing it, doing the spiritual thing, but some of the ones in the Whit race that have been doing this are taking that pendulum ride all the way to the other side. And now they are coming out and saying: we don't need Ascended Masters, we don't need any of the Angels, and I am the last word. So they are really getting off in their perception.

In one sense, well it is really hard to say, we don't want to judge it, but it's like the Black people have been saved from that kind of ego. Yet, they have suffered from the lack of a mainstream sort of linkage with spirit. And yet the White Race has ridden that ego to a level to where it is only going to hurt. They are also misleading some of their followers. There's all these things playing out, it's an amazing kind of melting pot, the Earth is and yet it is all going to work out.

Author's comment

Now will now take a look at what Sananda-Jesus had to say about the Black Race and His race during the time He walked the Earth as the man called Jesus. This is the first time that this information has come forth in this way and it is powerful. It will definitely stir up some denial, not only in the White Race but the Black Race as well and in many people of all races and religions. The thing about Black people is that some of them have been so mentally damaged that they can not and will not accept the possibility of having great historic figures such as Jesus or Moses being a part of the Black Race. This is a part of the greater reason why this information needs to come forward. Many things need to be in clear perspective. It is about the truth, not separation or pointing the blame at anyone. It all has a greater purpose than most could see or understand.

Address From Sananda-Jesus

Greetings to you, This is Sananda-Jesus and I speak to you from the heart energy, I speak to you from the heavens, I speak to you from love of the fifth dimension and I'm very much in tune with your desires to connect to the roots of your soul and the roots of the planetary soul. There are many aspects of the Earth presence that include the multi- dimensions of one's soul and that means that there are links, there are strands of energy to other aspects of Self throughout the universe. And when you hear people speak to you of your planetary roots in another part of the galaxy, you can be assured that this planetary root actually has a physical link, an energetic link into this Earth's presence. Your primary presence in the universe is now focused on the Earth. Yet, you have the ability to be multi-aware. That means that you can transfer your presence, transfer your consciousness to these other places or these other planets. And you have come into an awareness that is a very beautiful awareness of your multi- presence. And one of the goals in this incarnation for you and others who have deemed multi- awareness important, is to learn how to integrate and to experience the multi-awareness presence so that you can unify. The over all goals are to unify their soul, to unify the presence.

The roots of The man called Jesus

You have asked the channel about information that pertains to and concerns the dark skinned people and you know that I come from the dark skinned people. You know that I have been noticed and been from the dark skinned people. And the planet brought forth a variety of reasons of which I'm sure you are aware of, My presence, my message and many of the different aspects of myself have been molded to shape the views of what people think I should look like, and what people think I should have said, and what people think that I meant in terms of coming to this planet and the over all apparatus and the over all political situation should be. Indeed my presence was attributed as a political event rather than a spiritual event. This was in direct contradiction to what my mission was. My mission was not to be a political figure yet, I was made into a political figure. Therefore, there were various interpretations of how this political event should be played out in terms of forming different sects and how people claimed that this sect was the direct lineage of what my words were and also what my appearance was. So in truth, if my appearance was made known, there would be a great controversy. It would be a political event in itself. You may be surprised to know that 1 did not have a flowing beard as I was depicted. I did not have flowing hair as depicted but indeed looked more of what you would call the Semitic race at that time. More of the dark race on this planet. And it was certainly a fabrication about my color being other than dark skinned, but that is not really important.

My manifestation of image

What is important is the archetypical view that people have of a particular person. And if What is important is the archetypical view that people have of a particular person. And if people want to say that they have this view of me, indeed I have the ability to formulate my manifested Self into what people think would be most appropriate for me. Indeed it is true that when it comes time for the transition into the fifth dimension , or when it comes time for the transition into other realms through the death experience, a formulation of myself as an image does fit with what you are comfortable with. So for example, if you are comfortable with a flowing beard and a certain presence, then I am very comfortable in manifesting that form. And people will say then, what is your true form and I will say to you Anakhanda, what is your true form because you have a multi- presence on other planets, you have a presence on this planet. Which one is the real you? The real you is a light essence, the real you is an energy essence, the real you is a form that is in such a high vibration that to manifest a physical, or even an image, requires a step down in energy.

Roll of the dark skinned people on this planet

Let me say that you are very concerned and interested in the role and the teachings of the dark skinned people. The dark skinned people were the original people on this planet. They were the original inhabitants on this planet. They were the original developers of the evolution of the planet. They did come from various other planets but I would say to you that the important thing for you to remember is that the dark skinned people were the original genetic structural presence on the planet and when there was a genetic re- engineering that was brought down from another planet, it was with the dark skinned people that the genetic engineering begin. And it was the basic tools of the dark skinned people that were used to modify the presence and the views. And indeed when you look at the Pleiadians and when you look at others that have influenced the genetic structure of the planets, they were using the dark skinned people as there basic core structure. The role of the Ascended Masters that were of the Black Race, were great shamanistic leaders, and are great presences but have all been very much unknown, because they have been very much localized and they have not been willing to come forward.

Where are the Black Ascended Masters?

Anakhanda, you raised the question as to why are the dark skinned people not coming forward as Ascended Masters of certain spirituality. I would say to you that there has been such a down trodding, such damage to the ego and self-esteem that the people have not been able to develop strongly as a group. There are groups like yourself the Mushaba. Force, that are willing to reach out and unify and this will be forth coming because there is a huge consciousness, a large spiritual consciousness that's coming now and you are on the forefront of it. I send you now a blue and golden light into your aura and I activate your halo so that you can access all Ascended Masters from the Dark Skinned People.

Remember, that in a race that has been down trodden, there are inherited genetic blocks in spiritual development. These inherited spiritual blocks are really problems that can be overcome but, you must free the yoke of genetic blocks. You must free the yoke of past life energies that have transferred through the collective consciousness of your people. They are simply released, they are simply broken through and they are simply transcended and then there can be a huge awareness. I Sananda, send you my love and blessings for your powerful work, and know that you are going to reach many people and give them the message that they need to only transcend their collective blocks from their history. And to know that their true Ascended Masters will be coming forth. And let them know also that their teacher (Jesus) is a part of the Dark Skinned People. What ever might be told by the White people about my appearance, the truth is as you have heard it. And the truth is as you know that my true heritage in race is with the black skinned people. And it is not something that needs to be broadcast but it is something that needs to be understood. This is Sananda-Jesus, Blessings!

Author's Comments:

The above address is powerful and enlightening. A lot has been said and revealed about one of the greatest personages in the history of this world. It has been stated in his own words by his own spirit. I want to say that the comment that was made about manifesting to people in the image that they feel comfortable with is something that many people are unaware of. Most importantly, Spirit is colorless regardless of what cover we choose to wear when we come to the planet. Spirit does not get caught up into this color thing like people of Earth. Spirit is not concerned with the limited minds of humanity when it comes to what they should appear like to any particular individual. If you have been raised to believe that Jesus or some Master Teacher is a certain color or has a certain look, then when you pass into the finer dimensions or death, what ever you feel safe with will be there for you to see you through. It doesn't matter at that time what one appears as.

As people grow into greater understanding and awareness, the Light shall open up the Truth for all to see and to know for themselves. The reality is that when you are into the higher dimensions, there is no color anyway and for many beings, there is no form. Color and form is of the material concern. It is important that spirit does not add to the shock that many experience in death, as it is, by appearing in a form that people are not familiar with. The form that spirit manifests helps to bring comfort to the Spirit who has crossed over. And as far as the comment about the genetic blocks, it is something that Black people need not burden with and stuck with. As was stated, it can simply be overcome.

The fact that you bring awareness to this issue is enough to begin to disintegrate the blocks. It is something that each individual has to understand and as more understanding of this comes forth it will begin to change in the collective consciousness of the Black race as a whole. It only needs to reach a certain mass of change before all are affected. It is only to recognize that fact that as they see more and more Black people deeply involve and aware of the spiritual knowledge and see that the Black Race Ascended Masters are coming forward bringing the truth and history and the deeper spiritual knowledge. This alone will begin to erase the genetic blocks and the collective blocks from the consciousness. It simply needs to have light shed on it and it will take care of itself. It really is not a problem as was stated. As more and more people begin to and intend to become aware of their true spiritual heritage and lineage that is powerful enough to open it widely.

Chapter 3
The Black Race Origin And Other Historical Figures

We will open this chapter with an address from Ascended Master D. K. (Djwhal Khul). In his address, D.K. opened us up to information that was amazing and very in depth concerning the origin of the Black race and its mission. It was a very beautiful and inspiring address that uncovered a great deal of information that was not available before now. It really got things going in a powerful way. I can't say enough about what was said and how very grateful I am that he spoke of the things that he did. It really shed much light and love on this entire Black issue and opened up the path to a greater planetary healing to begin. Not only within the consciousness of the Black race but the White race and all races as well. This is an understanding that needs to be shared with all humanity. And to think that this is only the beginning of what will come forth to humanity from spirit, and particularly from the Ascended Realms, where the Black Race Ascended Masters will come and speak of their existence and why, until now, this knowledge was not available. Let us listen to the Master D.K.

MASTER D. K.

Blessings and greetings to you! I am Djwhal Khul and I sit with you in a counsel that we have created of love. I am very anxious to talk with you this day, I am very anxious to bring you information. I am anxious to smile with you and to meet with you and to speak with you. And I wish this day to re-acquaint you with information that perhaps has not been easily accessible, and yet it is some information very much about the Black race. Primarily, I would like to greet you and say to you in one sense the race of human kind upon the Earth was intended and is intended to be a "Rainbow Race". You may use that term in one way or another. I don't know if you use it in the way that I use it so I will explain. When I speak about a Rainbow Race, I speak about a unity. For in the rainbow that you see in the sky, there is not one arch that is above any other nor is there an arch that can be separated out from other arches. It is the completion; it is the whole insertion program of each arch that compiles the rainbow that brings the brightness of many destinies. It brings the brightness of many attributes and very many colors. And so I would say to you, the rainbow expression is very deep within the heart and the mind of many Masters and those who over light the Earth.

As we have said in prior discussions, the race primarily called the Black race comes from a seeding of extra-terrestrial races that came from places outside of the Earth. In fact, the term extra- terrestrial denotes extra, beyond the Earth terrain. And I would say that every race and all races and all peoples that live now upon the earth have extra-terrestrial seeds within the peoples. For it was a certain agreement to bring forth many seeds and bring them to the Garden of Eden of the Earth. And therefore, the rainbow was built with seeds of diversity for the actual purpose and the one plan of the Earth which was to come back into oneness, reflect oneness through a certain diversity, through a myriad of rainbow rays, through a myriad of frequencies, that would all work together not alone but all in one and reflect God in a myriad of ways. Well, as you know, and as we have said, considerably many of the races have come from Sirius, but then there were others that came from other dimensions and other galaxies that do not allow, or cannot bring forth a name, through the mind of the channel. I would like to bring to you a little settling of this kind of information.

There are many veils around the Earth. There have been many distortions and much confusion in the physical dimensions of the Earth. Therefore, a lot of the information has been withheld because it could not penetrate the veils of distortion, confusion, fear and suppression that go along with what has happened on the face of the Earth. We lay no blame and yet we say to you that much of the desired information will be forth coming but has been withheld because of the pre-judgments of humanity, because of the ignorance of humanity, the choice to ignore, and because of all the pain and confusion that is placed up and pinned in veils very thickly around certain knowledge and around certain understandings. Therefore, I would say to you, that all information that comes down about Creation on Earth and information of the races on the Earth, has little loop holes in it and all of it has certain circles that are not filled in, gaps in other words. We hope that in this session and in days to come, with many more sessions that more and more information will come through and the channels will be open.

We would also like to say at the onset that the channel has no prejudice. The channel is not prejudice against any race. But even if the channel has no prejudice, it maybe at a loss to bring forward certain information that has been covered with what you might call the dust of time, the dust of humanity. In fact, many great channels throughout time immemorial have not been able to access certain of the records. I would like to say that the Akashic records are not easily accessible and there has been a decision that certain information and a need to know this information, would come up from within the beings themselves in order to assist in the release of said information. Therefore, I would say to you that you are correct in assuming that there is a lot of information that has not reached the masses about many things and also about the Black race and its beginnings upon the Earth and the African lineage and all of that, because of the tremendous lack of love and the distortions and the divisions that have taken place upon the Earth. It is almost as if smoke has risen into the heavens and into the firmaments to block the sight of many. And yet, there are many things that can be known and will be known so have patience.

The uncovering and this recovering has a lot to do with the remembrances, has a lot to do with re-alignment, has a lot to do with reintegration of those categories and those memories and all of it shall come to light as the ascension of the Earth comes into it's grand finale, it's grand beginning, its middle and all of its stages that are coming on line. Suffice it to say that there are many categories of Masters that are, what you would call with the black skin, or having presented themselves with the black skin. I would like to back up and also say here to those of us in the heavens and to those of us in the Ascended realms, it matters not what is the color of the skin is for we are about unity and we are about oneness. We will not be about separation, but we do understand the sentiments of the heart and we do understand the pain of division and we do understand the pain of not being able to build the tapestry having lost many of the threads and we understand that information is wisdom and that wisdom heals.

When soul takes on a body

We would like to bring to your attention that when ever a Soul takes on a body and comes into an extended body in physicality that, that is simply an extension and an expression of that Soul. And I would say that many Souls are groups with many extensions belonging to the group consciousness of the Soul and have brought through a body that has come through in many different colors or what you would call races.

For instance, take the energy of Isis that has been known as a Black Princess, a Black Goddess, and as the Goddess of Nature. And it is the same essence as is the essence of Mother Mary. And there is some confusion as to whether Mary was Black, is Isis Black. Isis has been known as a Black Angel, as a Black Female Goddess, and as a magician. In fact, the symbol of Isis is Sirius itself, which is one of the lineages of the Black races on Earth? And yet, the Mother Mary brought forth her expression and it is not seen as Black and yet is it or is it not?

Many of these have been veiled and yet, the energy of Mother Mary has come through in all of the races. Coming through as QuanYin for it was the same or is the same Soul energy. (Here it is saying plainly that Mother Mary and QuanYin are one and the same Soul expressed in different races on Earth). So know that Soul gives birth to the extensions of the Souls that take incarnation. Understand that it is the energy of the Soul that is the most important. Yet we understand that to those living out lifetimes and incarnations on the Earth, it is the recognition of the extension of the Soul that is very important and so, we shall speak.

People of the rays

I would like to say that every race that has lived itself out in it's diversity on the Earth plane has a certain connection to the rainbow and to the stars. I don't know if you remember but I spoke to you one time about the seven rays. I would like to say that a race of humanity comes forth under that banner of the rainbow and under that banner of the rainbow ray of the seven rays, and each race encapsulates or embraces certain ray qualities. Primarily the Black race as it came to be known on the Earth came forth to master the qualities of the first ray. What is the first ray? I will review that it is the ray of God's power. The first ray called the blue ray, sometimes called the red ray-closer into the Earth, is sometimes called the blue ray-further out, galactically. It is the ray of God's will, it is the ray of faith, it is the ray of power, and it is a very strong ray. The Black race encompasses two rays, the first ray and the seventh ray, and I would say to you, that in the beginning and in the end, first and last, alpha and omega embraced the Black race. What is the seventh ray? It is the violet ray and the characteristics of the seventh ray are freedom, justice, absolute victory and mercy. It is the ray of St. Germain. The Black race as it came forth and was seeded on the Earth mastering for the position and for the purpose of mastering the qualities of power and freedom, came forth both as a Blue race and as a

Violet race. In fact, the Original Black Race had a little tone, a little tint, a hint of blue in the black and violet in the colors as well. It was a Blue race and a Violet race and those colors showed up in the aura and they showed up in the skin.

I draw your attention to early Lemuria. I draw your attention to the high civilization living on the continent of Africa during the time of Lemuria. It was a Blue race and a Violet race and it was the race that you call the Black race. The Lemurians that lived there adhered very well to the science of the spoken word. They were very verbal, they were very expressive. All of the races came forth from the Rays. Keep that in mind. Keep in mind that violet is freedom and the blue ray is the power ray, all the true colors and rays of the rainbow of God. But no longer is there any pure color in the aura or in the skin of any race on earth. Why? Because of distortions, because of confusions, because of divisions. Every nation has its calling; every race has its destiny of that which it chooses to portray.

And in truth from the Ascended perspective, all the races need to come together and embrace one another, put an end to division and be like the rays. Be absolutely like the rainbow, embracing, connected to one another. For the truth is beloved, there is no such thing as division. There are divisions that are created by ignorance, by misunderstandings, and misperceptions. From the point of God, there are no divisions, there is all this oneness, there's unity, why? Because the threads of unity exist as threads in a tapestry and all are uniquely connected and interlocked. It cannot be that they are separated and yet they chose a kind of distorted version which divides and conquers and sets division within. It is all because of certain energies that came to the earth that created a decline, and that created a certain vulnerability that divided.

Extra-Terrestrial Races -Personal agenda-Division

Let us say that it wasn't the original intention but within free will, many came to the Earth. When certain Extra-terrestrial races came, when certain brotherhoods and sisterhoods came to the Earth, they may have had certain agendas, they may have sung out in a loud voice, and others had the free will to listen. Therefore, certain division was brought here by invaders. Certain aliens brought through certain distortions and certain confusions and set certain traps, why? Because they had personal agendas, they wanted to do something. Let us say that certain invaders brought certain seeds of deception that had a little destruction, to the Blue race. All of this was allowed because of free will. For where there was a strength of conviction there could have been a choice not to mix and to mingle with the invaders, but to kind of hold up those stories that came through to a certain measurement that would not have distorted. And yet the distortions came in and the confusion and some might say well it was the plan all along, to bring in distortion and come back to oneness from polarity, come back to oneness from division. Who is to say? Perhaps it is that I would like to leave that question. It is a question that life needs to answer. Distortions did come in to the land of Africa where these Blue and Violet races were seeded. Distortions came in and certain sacred rituals were kind of watered down. Certain judgments came in, certain rituals were distorted. Certain energies came in such as voodoo, such as sacrifices, and certain things that were not really inherent in the race. Certain fears and thought forms took form and there were certain divisions that came about and then there was the need to protect against divisions, and there were a need to turn fear into protection. And the truth is that many of the beings turned their attention away from God, away from oneness and unity and away from the very precepts of the blue and the violet determinations or the race destiny. The people became vulnerable. The nation did become divided and you might say that certain superstitions came in with certain practices because of the dilution of focus. As the people became vulnerable, they became more and more susceptible to divisions. When there is vulnerability then an entrance of many things, entities, precepts, that are foreign to one's original thought, can come in and take root. In other words, when someone becomes very vulnerable they can become divided and a nation became divided. When such division came in, it came in by the way to all races, not just the Black race or the Blue or Violet race. All of the races had a certain impurity that entered as manipulations and dark regimes, and controls happened upon the face of the Earth. We might say that the mother earth thought that she might be able to handle it, but it wasn't Mother Earth!

The beings living in Lemuria and Atlantis and the early civilizations thought they could stay true to their original doctrines and allow certain laggard races to enter the Earth, those who needed a planet. And yet, it was like the snake in the Garden of Eden kind of whispering, certain information that created a certain division. Interestingly enough, on the continent of Africa, as division set in, it set in amongst the people living there and they began to divide themselves. They divided against themselves, against each other within themselves, parts of themselves turning against other parts, dividing a little bit away from God and Spirit, getting a little diluted, you might say. They divided you might say on color lines. Interestingly enough, they themselves began to divide along the lines of color. And you might say; "well why was this?" Why is color so important? And it is because of difference and diversity. Because like we have said, many are compiled of what you might call the Black race, the Violet race, the Blue race and many seedings from many places, not just from Sirius but beyond. And they held with them a certain memory of difference, a little memory of having come from a different place. And in a climate of division, those little sparks of difference within add up. It isn't a negative thing, we are not speaking good or bad, right or wrong, we are simply speaking out, giving a little look into a picture.

You might say that the people living there lost a little bit of their inner spiritual stronghold with the conflict of the inner and outer, and inner conflict and outer conflict between races and tribes. There was also a conflict between what was inside each one, should I do this or should I do that, will I do this, will I do that? They became divided within themselves and outside of themselves, and many times it was because of color. It is easier to look outside than inside. And part of the choice of learning for the Planet Earth was not to be caught up on the outside of things, not to give the power outside, not to take power from outside, but to find the power inside, the sanctuary of God. Therefore, there has been for a very long time, a certain knowledge and set of lessons that have to do with inside and outside, between looking at the outside of things, the color of things, the skin of things, and looking at the inside of things, the heart of the matter. When anger comes forth from division, from battle, from confusion, and from distortion, then it is a misuse of the threefold flame. Then either love, wisdom or power begin to lessen and that is what happened here and it is also what happened everywhere on the earth with all of humanity. The threefold flame in the heart, love, wisdom, and power, began to get smaller as anger and diffusion, confusion and distortion entered into the physical dimensions. Many traps were set and many fell into the traps. Alright, bare in mind that the main precept of the race called the Black race, originally the Violet and the Blue race, was to develop love for each other in a path of sisterhood and brotherhood. Interestingly enough, the Black race call each other brother and sister. Why did they start doing that? When did it begin? You might ask the question, but I will say that the root of it is in the very precept and path of determination and destiny. For it was at its core to develop a love for each other that could not be divided, not be divided along color lines, outside lines, but that the heart would be the eyes that saw no difference between anyone. It was a path of brotherhood and sisterhood.

Author's Comment

I would like to say here that I find it very interesting that the precept was brotherhood and sisterhood and that naturally, the Black race call each other brother and sister. Can it be, that on an unconscious level we are tapping into what our path and teachings were really about? Could it be that we are seeking to express our nature that extends to all people, that of being brother and sister? I find that many of the Black race calls many other races brother and sister as well! What is that saying? What does it all mean? Let's continue on to see where the root of this came from.

<u>D.K. continue An Ascended Being Called Afra</u>

I would like to bring to your attention the high civilization that lived on the continent of Africa. I would like to also bring to your attention the being called "AFRA" called "The Patron of Africa." Africa was named after the being called Afra, and some may have considered this to be the first Black Ascended Master, and so the ears perk up here! Over 500,000 years ago, there was a Being living on the continent you call Africa, and this Being was a Black Ascended Master who achieved ascension and came to the Earth to show the way, to show a way. One thing that he came to show was that the only true slavery is the slavery within, slavery to the mind, to confusion and to the lack of unity. Alright, Afra was a very important being. You wonder about the name and the name comes from the word frater, which means brother in Latin. And this Being was immensely humble because this Being was so expanded and evolved. But he did not want anyone to relate to him on any pedestal. He simply said that I am your brother, call me Afra, for it means a brother, I am a brother. Interesting, is it not, for even now the Black race refers to each other as brothers and sisters. I draw your attention to this Being who came to show a path of brotherhood in a world, in a nation, with a calling for freedom and for power, where division had set in and conquering had set in, and division amongst themselves had set in where each one would go against the other and fight against each other; Black races fighting against each other.

Afra came to show a path of brotherhood. Beloved One, He was a Christ. He held the energy of the state of Being called the Christ. He came to deliver the message of a Christ. He came to show the path of brotherhood and sisterhood, of unity, and like many Christ's after him and before him, he was killed. He was actually crucified, I believe, although the records on that are not clear, but he was killed. His passion was for freedom and he wanted everyone to understand the truth of the meaning of being a brother and a sister on the path. The path that he referred to was the path of the Holy Spirit. And what he referred to was the freedom that would come about, that does come about, when true and full unity dissolves all the differences. You can say that certain forces and invasions and interferences came in to the people living there. Certain oppressions came forth, oppressions from the outside that lead to each one oppressing each other. And the beings were forced from without to do this or to do that, that which they would normally not do. And then inaccurate, untrue, and a lowered sort of consciousness came forth from inside them as well. You might say that there was decline and the opposite of that would be what? Transcendence, and yet on the path of learning within the learning curve, there was the lesson of decline, the loss of some spirituality that had been known and had been gained.

Alright, the main gift is to find the inner light temple inside. The main lesson is to go into the inner sanctuary no matter what is happening on the outer. The main understanding that was lost was the advancement on the path of initiation that takes place on the inner, that does have a connection to the rays and yet all the rays are one. The understanding being, that freedom and equality must go beyond color, color within a race and color within other races. Because the way that God views races is simply a human race, that they are one.

Another lesson is the inner success verses the outer success. Because you can win freedom and equality on the outer, but it needs to go deeper and be deep seated all the way into the inner. What I want to say now is that color is outer. The focus on color is outer, whether it is by a Black race, a White race a Yellow race, or a Red race.

The African people and their descendants are very, were very and continue to be very, very, very wealthy in spirit. Some of this has been lost. It is our attempt in this meeting to restore some of that information, to let you know there is Black Ascended Masters, to let you know there are Masters and Soul energies that has come forth in Black skin and also in White skin. There is a soul extension of the energy of Jesus that wore the Black skin and also of Moses. In fact, there have been cycles of those souls that have come forth. In fact, there is some confusion as to which Christ there was, for there were many that walked the face of the earth. The important thing to remember was that the first being to make his ascension was Afra, if you consider the Black race, and that being returned many times to sponsor what you might call a very strong, elegant and mighty people. He never wanted fame, glory or anything. He simply wanted to restore the original focus of the Blue race and the Violet race.

Please know that in Lemuria and in the advance civilizations of Africa, it was a spiritually advanced kind of world, very advanced and those advancements are held in the genetic codes of Africans, whether they are African Americans or Africans living in Africa, held within the cellular memories and they shall come forth. I would say that perhaps the missing trait, the trait that got lost throughout certain time frames in those peoples, was the trait of brotherhood and sisterhood. You might say, "but that is such our strong hold." It is your stronghold now as the race is recovering its memory.

But, please remember that the race itself divided amongst itself and it was almost like Cain and Able, in that Cain took his arm up against his brother, yes he did, he slew his brother. This is being corrected in all of humanity as each one turns toward the other.

The Ascended Master Afra is the overseer of a certain genetic code introduced to Africa. I would say that the origin of this Master was from another world, from another planet, not really from Africa and that the language took on a meaning of its own. (This being is from Planet Mushaba) In other words, perhaps his name was really a different name than what is called Afra. But enough similarity would go forth to create this one, and his energy, kind of like that of Beings that over light a whole galaxy, beings that over light a country, a continent, and a nation.

There are Angels who over light clusters, and living galaxies. And so there was a passage of information or vibration that came to this one whose origins are where? The origin of that, Master do you know what the origin, the divine heritage of a seed of God is? It is very, very deep, very, very far; it is like a drop in an ocean that then moves into streams of many different lifetimes. And so, if you go back to the origin of the drop, it comes from the sea of extreme potentiality, it comes from a formless sea, it comes from creation, and it comes from the creator. So, that current, that frequency came into alignment as the Ascended Master Afra. Maybe Afra is not the right word, maybe not the real name, but similar enough to have picked up some of the energy of that frequency of vibration of a name. Let us say that in some ways there are two Afra's. There is the energy that was much larger, more like a group consciousness, and then there was the life stream.

I want you to think of Sananda for a moment. Everyone is familiar with Sananda. They are also familiar with the life time known as Jesus and the lifetime known as, I believe it is Tyana of Apollonius. Well there are many lifetimes of Jesus and some of them are being withheld because they almost aren't meant to be shared and because it might cause a little rift in different religions. He really walked through and across almost all the religions, and everyone has there own guide, there own God, there own role model. They do not want to see Jesus in the Buddha tradition. And so some things are just not quite being revealed. But Jesus had many lifetimes in which he came. And yet there is an aspect that is beyond Jesus, that is beyond Sananda, even beyond that, and there is another name for an even larger entity of that kind of group or life stream, and this is what we mean.

Also, I would say to you to meditate upon the Ascended Master Afra in his Ascended Master form or in a greater form where he may have been overseeing a little bit more of the beginnings of the Earth Origins, kind of the Father, the Father of Africa in a sense. There is an angelic quality, by the way, to that, which embodied the whole of Africa.

Speaking to the council

Alright, well I said that I would speak to the Councils about arranging a certain exercise with a Black Race Master and I would say that I would like for you in your heart beloved one, to begin to call to the Master Afra yourself. Perhaps there is a time when the channel can channel him, perhaps they will choose to, perhaps you will choose the channel to, but perhaps you yourself can begin to open to that energy and directly ask for the infusion of wisdom, light, connection and information to come into the cone above the crown to come into your dialog during your night time of sleep and during your meditations. Let us say that we have gone to the Councils, we have opened up some lines of communications, we have allowed a little bit of information to trickle through, have we not? And I would say that in your near future you will be a receiver of that information. Ask Afra to speak to you directly. Sit with pen in hand, meditate, let go of any control, let go of any anticipation, let go of expectation, let go of what you want to hear and of what you don't want to hear, let go of anything that would interfere. Be free, be clear, be conscious, and be open to see what comes through. Ground yourself and call to spirit. It is important at this time to always request spirit. Ask for the Angels that primarily work with the Black race to come around you. Ask for the Blue race, the Violet race, and ask for those Angels as well. Call forth to the Being called Isis. Call forth to the Being called Thoth, many of the energies like Zoroaster and Thoth and some of the Egyptian Beings. Even if you were to see their portraits, their paintings on the walls, and on the scrolls, you would see that they had some of the African physical attributes. And that they were themselves a blend of African and Egyptian. Ask Them to be with you. Call to the Master Muhammad, and call to many Masters back to the Mushaba Force.

They Came From Many Universes

You were told that before the Black Race was on Sirius that they came from another universe. Well yes! There are many universes and numerous, numerous millions of galaxies, yes it is true! There is a mixing, there is a blending and the Black race known as the Blue and Violet race in truth, had seeds that did come from other galaxies, from other systems and it is true. The name of those galaxies is hard to bring through nor could the sound be brought though, for it is extremely difficult coming from another universe. It is almost as if it is as different as different can be. And the channel is not capable at this time of bringing through those sounds or those qualities. I would say to you that it doesn't really matter where they came from only that they came from the huge, huge map of God.

About the first universe where Black people came from before Sirius, it isn't that they really came from a first universe, they came from somewhere in the galaxy I would say, some other planets, different planets. In fact, the Black race is made up of not just those who came from Sirius which is a star system, so we are talking about the same universe. Let me make it clear, same universe. So it isn't really that they left the first universe and went to another universe, they literally, well lets say, the Black race all came from this local current Universe that you associate as the Universe, that you call the Universe. There are other parts to it, smaller ones attached and so forth. So it wasn't that it was another universe, but it is the universe as you know it, and think of it, and acquire knowledge upon it, and investigate it. It's a lot, a lot, a lot larger than what you currently put value on and so I just wanted to clear that up.

All the races are a myriad. Think of it as an ocean; think of it as the ocean of God and cup fulls, and cup fulls, and cup fulls enter the ocean to pick up soul families, with soul agreements, with soul versions, with soul communities, and with soul unities. Think of the little drops of water as all of the different beings that come out of the souls, that take incarnation, and they are vast. Because the ocean is the vastest, inclusive of all that is. And the cups are many, and they move through this ocean. The particles, meaning the little drops of water, have been taken up through absorption and come down through the rain of clouds. I would say that there is the remote possibility that every world has a little segment, or fragment of segments, and fragments too numerous to name. You are a fragment of God and you shall return into the unity that is God that knows no separation and never intended it. And the important thing is that the temple of unity is within and no matter how much oppression comes from the outside to any race, each race has a purpose to unify through the temple of oneness from within to unify to the without, to love, to bless, to forgive and to reassemble the tapestry of oneness.

All races had oppression and slavery

It doesn't matter who was the oppressor, or who was the oppressed. Blacks have oppressed other Blacks, Whites have oppressed Blacks, Whites have oppressed many races and White's have been oppressed in this world and in other worlds. Oppression is ignorance Slavery has been on the Earth since before the time of Atlantis. Extra-terrestrials with higher knowledge, and little knowledge, and dwarf knowledge of love have suppressed races that were big of heart, but little of knowledge. Slavery is not new and it is not new to the Black race. In fact, the Black Races have enslaved their own races and the White Races have enslaved their own races. The Atlanteans developed a race of slaves and some extra-terrestrials wanted to enslave the entire human race for a very long time. Slavery is a distortion of love and of unity. It is a private agenda. It is an agenda outside of God's agenda. It is a confusion and a distortion. And it always distorts no matter who is involved.

Evolved Black Beings take all traces with them

You asked the question: Those of the Black race who left the Earth, why did they take with them all traces, all knowledge of their connection to the stars?

(A). Because of their own understanding of diffusion, delusion, and distortion, they did it to protect. They thought that it was a protection of that knowledge and they decided that they would return at the appropriate time when the minds of men were open, and the forgiveness energies were flowing and the heart lead the mind. Then they would be bringing those traces and that knowledge that would unite, rather than divide, and would not get diluted but would remain in fullness.

Why didn't the Spiritual Councils get involved?

You asked why didn't the Spiritual Councils do anything to bring awareness to the Black people's situation? Well the answer is this: the people themselves a long time ago got distorted. They made some choices that weren't so clear. They were also invaded upon, they were interfered with. Manipulations have come into every single race on the Earth. Manipulations of the reptilian agenda, manipulations of many races that wanted to rule the earth. We do not fault any color skinned people. And the Spiritual Councils cannot interfere when people make choices, because of free will. And if a down heartedness, a lost of inspiration occurs within and amongst the people, it is not that the Angels can simply go in. The Angels were always there but sometimes the voice of diffusion, the voice of confusion and distortion speaks louder. The voice that says look at the outside rather than the inside has spoken very loudly on the Earth and all have suffered. Spiritual Councils did not sit by and do nothing. They always sent a leader. They sent Afra into Africa and yet he was killed. I cannot see who killed him, nor can I access at this point, the means by which he was killed, but it does look like it was a crucifixion or something like that. In other words, many people have made many choices in their process of bringing back the light of understanding. The Spiritual Councils are not at fault. Within the doctrines of free will they can not impose. They understand, and have patience with that which you call time. In fact, time does not live in the Higher Realms. It lives in the way that you view it on Earth. Therefore, the patience to outlive time, to out weigh time, to out wait the time that brings forth the circle, that comes full circle, that then rekindles the desire to know, the desire for one candle to light the other candles and to bring back awareness, to resurrect, to realign, and to reinsert, and to recalibrate, and to again ascend in consciousness. Perhaps it is that the Councils knew that, that the resurgence and the fire would be rekindled, is being rekindled, and would then come back on line. Believe me, beloved one, the energies are still held in cellular memories and all was never lost.

Black Ascended Masters serve on the Councils of Light.

We have talked to you about your question about Black Race Ascended Masters. Many were from Egypt; many were from the energies within the Middle East. Many were from that which you call the continent of Africa. The ones that are famous are perhaps Isis, perhaps Thoth, perhaps some of the pharaohs and some of the descendants of them, who were Ascended Beings. You ask, do any of them serve on the Councils of Light and do they interact with any of the other Ascended Masters? In the Ascended Realms there is no division. The Master Afar serves right there along with Kuthumi, along with El

Morya. There is an Ascended Master who is Black by the name of Sophia, and there is an Ascended Master aspect of El Morya that is Black. Many of the Ascended have aspects of their soul that have come in as Black Beings and have Ascended. This is just not known. But in the Councils that work upon human kind, of course there is no division. They interact freely with each other. The aspect of Isis that is Black and the aspect of Mary that was considered White and the aspect of Quan Yin, are all the same Soul, and they work together and serve together, whether you know it or not. We understand that you want to make sense of all of this.

Psychological damage to both Black and White

We understand, because you said that it seems like a plan was involved, concerning the Black issue, not only here on Earth but also in the dimensions, as above so below. Yes, we understand that very deep, psychological damage has been done to the minds of the Black people, we understand that. But we also say to you, that deep, untold, psychological damage has also been done to the minds of the White people. Whether one is the oppressor or the oppressed, the deep psychological damage is there. In fact, you might say that a certain sense of purity is more instilled in the one who is inflicted, and a little less purity, as time prevails, in the one who is the inflictor. Let us say, that sometimes if you consider karma and you consider the living out of experiences, the deepest and hardest karma would be for those who have killed. And those who have been caught up in the killing and in the atrocity, perhaps, they have a karma as well, to live out, a balance to achieve. But the balance that is karma is much heavier for those who are the oppressors, even more then those who are oppressed.

Author's Comment:

I would like to comment on the above. It is interesting to me that Master D. K. mentioned that damage is done to the inflictor as well as the inflicted. This is something that people should understand. I used to say too many people that the White race has a problem mentally to feel that they are superior to the Black race or any race. It is damaging to the children to be raised up with those kinds of ideals and beliefs instilled in them, that they are better, superior etc. I always thought that it was a mental problem for anyone to feel that way. There is definitely damage done to both involved and I see the sense in the inflictor having a deeper damage done. To be that kind of person with that kind of hatred and mentality it has to take its toll. It has to weigh heavily on the soul. I look at many people of the White race and they are so unconscious of how they respond to Black people. It is a normal response to them and they do not even see it. They do not realize that there is this certain attitude that is present and they do not see it for themselves. That is, some of them, because it is true that there are those who know exactly what they are doing. But then too, the Black people have to take a look at themselves as well. There is a certain attitude there when it comes to being around and dealing with White people. Both attitudes seem to feed off each other. This is not with all Whites or with all Blacks or with all of any race. But it is something that needs to be looked at by all. Let us continue with the Master D. K's address:

The power of color

Ascended Masters of Color - Ascended Beings of Light

The truth, beloved, is that if you go back, back far enough, you will see that the Black Race has also been oppressors. Every race on earth has taken both sides and played them all. We understand the references that you are speaking of about the bad guys wear black. We understand certain of the influences you talk about, the angel food cake is white and the devils food cake is black, the angel of death is dark and wearing dark robes and the angels of love and peace are white, wearing white robes.

Note: I addressed those things mentioned above because it always gives reference to Black as being something bad. This will be further looked at in one of the proceeding chapters. Let us continue.

We also understand that color is a very interesting thing. For in India when someone gets married they wear red. And yet in the west when someone gets married, often times they wear white and they would consider it a blasphemy to wear red. That is to some more of a sexual more of a sort of lower carnal color. But in India, it is not. It is a sign of love, and it is also a color of power. I also draw your attention to the fact that nuns wear black and to the fact that priests wear black and that often times black is considered the color of divinity. So there is a very large cross section of the assignment of colors in the form of clothing, in the form of tapestry and it is different for every culture, very different. Yet in the culture that is considered the White culture there has been a certain upholding of the white standing for purity. Please understand that the title, Great White Brotherhood, the white refers to the white light that is the prism of the seven rays. Remember the Blue and the

Violet race ray has to do with a mixture or admixture of all the properties of all the colors which when you mix them all together, comes into white. Absence of color is generally noted as black. In one sense, the absence of color in all colors is very much the same. I would also like to draw your attention to a very high ray that is called the blue/black ray. It is a very high ray, a very deep galactic ray.

Distortions and stories need to be fixed.

And so, I would draw your attention to the fact that all of that is a distortion that is not true and if it causes serious problems among Black people, it is because of the loss of information, the disinformation and misinformation. Perhaps it is you, and others like you, who can bring back the information that none of that is true and that all of that has been used to kind of bring about a loss of spirit in the people. We understand that there is a lack of self-esteem. We understand that most of the incarcerated beings on the Earth are Black and are Black males. We understand that there is a fear amongst White people of Black people and we understand that there is a fear amongst Black people of White people and we understand that the distortions have gone very deep. We understand that certain stories were passed on and they created the fears that came alive in children. Children don't have those fears, they are taught many distortions. Therefore, the only way to move out of distortions, without pointing fingers is to embrace love, embrace unity, forgive and bring back the understanding of how it all happened in the first place. It's that when one looks to the outside of things instead of the inside of things, distortions come in. We understand that the morale of the Black race in America for instance has been low. We understand that many things have gone forth. Many leaders have come out of those neighborhoods. And there is a renaissance of feeling but we understand that there is a long way to go.

Controllers of the Earth

We understand that there is still a group that controls the Earth, the Illuminati, the secret government. And they are not the Blacks. They are more of what you call the Whites and so we understand the controls that are still prevalent. All of this is understood in the Heavens and all of this is being attended to. The Ashtar Command, the Spiritual Hierarchy's Divine infiltration that is being planned and the Divine intervention and all the Forces of Light are being sent onto the Earth to reawaken, to realign, and reintegrate everyone into their spiritual lineage, their spiritual heritage. We understand that you have noted many things. We understand clearly those who orchestrated those beliefs. Think of it as the Controllers, think of it as the ones who control the finances in your world, the government in your world, the ones who create the drugs, and then put them out on the street and then arrest the ones who take the drugs, who buy the drugs. They sell it to them and they arrest them for taking the drugs. There are rulers, and I call them dark rulers, but they do not have dark skin for the most part. These rulers have negative Extraterrestrial origins. They are very much in control of the Earth and they perpetuate and they propagate untrue myths and stories and orchestrate concepts. Therefore, the people must understand this. They must acquaint themselves with the secret government, and secret plans and doctrines, and the indoctrinations, and the propagation of misinformation. They must acquaint themselves in many ways with what has been a missed perception. And yet, they must not blame the entire White race. Because it isn't true, it didn't come from all of the White race. In fact, I would say that most of the race is not even guilty. Maybe they are guilty of holding misperceptions that were handed down to them generation after generation. Every misperception stores in the genetic bundles in the cellular memory. Therefore, it is not their fault. There are very few who control the purse strings, the economies and the wars upon your Earth. All of this is in the process of change. All of this shall soon be delivered and an exodus shall soon take place.

Closing remarks by Master D. K.

Please call to Moses. Moses had Black blood. There is a mixture in the blood of Moses and there are many veils surrounding that. But I would say that he had a lot of Black blood, although he may also have had some different strings of blood. He is a Master who is very much in charge of transfiguration and the law of the One. Love shall set everyone free, and we hope that we have shed a little bit of light on this subject. Please understand that some of the Black magic did originate in Africa. Some of the Voodoo practices did originate there when the true knowledge got diffused and distorted. It is best that the past not be referenced, for the future is bright. Reference the past for understanding, forgiveness and love and be an example. Let us bless the Golden Race, the Christ race, the Race of all races that will supercede all that has happened upon the earth. Understand the choice of every soul prior to birth to come into the family, the race and the situations that they chose. Understand this and bare in mind the original pursuits, power and freedom that the Blue and Violet race chose to depict and to decode on the face of the Earth. Victory shall be the name of the game! Amen, Amen, Amen, and Amen.

Master Kuthumi speaks on Ascended Master Afra

First, let me say that the Ascended Masters of the Black Origin are very linked to Sananda/Jesus and they are very linked with the Christ light and they are very linked with the entry of life force of the human consciousness into Africa. Afra is one of the Ascended Masters that is the Oversoul, Seer of the continent of Africa, as well as the Oversoul, Seer of the first genetic codes that were introduced into Africa when the Adam species was activated. So he is one of the primordial souls of the African continent, and Afra is the primordial soul energy of the Black people that entered in the times of the introduction into the continent. Now, this activation occurred on a very profound level at that time of introduction. The Oversoul of Afra is very taxed at this time because of the huge tragedies and deaths that are occurring on the Continent of Africa and the souls of the African people are in extreme danger because of these deaths.

The Goddess Light Energy

Afra is also manifested as a Goddess light Energy in the teachings of the ancient tribes. For the original connection with the soul and spirit was in the Goddess

Energy, and I think you know that already. It was the Goddess Energy that was first responsible for the bringing of spiritual consciousness to the peoples in the Continent of Africa. You have seen these statues of Women Goddesses. This was the introduction of the spiritual light. It was not about Multi-Gods or that the spirituality was very primitive but it was also very experiential and this is one of the gifts of Black people, their spirituality. You can talk about the intellectual aspects of spirituality but the Black people have brought forth the experience of spirituality in a direct way. They have been able to be into the 4th and 5th dimensions, go into trances, and go into the dimensional corridors immediately.

Ascended Master Sophia

There is an Ascended Master and her name is Sophia. She is very powerful and she is very little known and you can call and ask to be around her. She lived upon the Earth and she ascended. In your world and on your planet and within all the different races and all the civilizations in history for a very long time, the feminine quality has been omitted. The truth is at the level of what you would call God. There is a Female God and a Masculine God. An aspect that is exactly equal. It is a unity. So please know that even at the head of your Universe at this time, and a very short time ago came a feminine figure, very few know about. What I can say in this space and time is that she is an Ascended Master working within the first ray, but not exclusively. Remember, separation accounts for much upon the Earth and in the Heavens but in the Higher Realms oneness accounts for everything. Sophia is a very strong energy, a very protective kind of maternal energy and yet very much the energy of strength and will, and wisdom.

African Drums and Ceremonies

So we give into the beauty of the African drums, the beauty of the Ancient African ceremonies that had intense power. So the connection with Afra is made by you and others through the experience of these drums, through the experience of the dances and not necessarily through the intellectual ways or mental ways. It is important that the message get out about the purpose of the African peoples message which was specific information to share about the primordial energy that came forth on the Earth and the intention of that energy within the African continent to bring Enlightenment to the Earth. Remember, that Jesus was Black and so when you ask about Black or lets say Dark Skinned Masters if you wish, that he was a Black Race Ascended Master.

Chapter 4
Psychological damage and its effects

This is a subject of great depth and those who are affected by it which is basically everyone on the earth in some way or another. They must be very open with themselves in acceptance of that which is truth. Many times people do not like to admit to being affected in an adverse way. They always want to be in control. They must understand that being affected by things in an adverse way does not in any way make you less or make you one who is judged. It is a reality that most people are affected in a psychological way. Whether it is what has been or is being done to them or by what they have done or one is doing to someone else. This also include what is being said to them or what they are saying to someone else. Psychological effects are very damaging and can lead to a great deal of other problems that show themselves in many different ways. A big problem with many is the fact that they do not even think, consider or know that they are affected.

Psychological Damage through Slavery

Lets take a look at the psychological damage that has been done to Black people as a race as the result of slavery. Slavery was about much more than physical slavery. It was about having a lasting effect throughout time that would affect Black people for generations upon generations. It was about it being instilled in the genetics and the DNA of a people so much so, that they could never get away from it, at least in a psychological way. It created deficiencies of self-worth and self-value which entails a very long list of things. It affects the mind in ways, from being settled to being overwhelmed. Let's see some of the many ways that the Black race has been affected and damaged in a psychological and mental sense. Many of the problems that Black people are experiencing today are from the effects of slavery and so are the problems of the White race, but this will be handled separately. You must really look and observe very carefully at the actions and the reasons why someone acts the way they do. You must look at the root cause of the circumstances to get to the answer.

Psychological damage is something that runs deep within the mind and psyche of a person, many levels deep. It controls people actions, attitudes, characteristics, mind set and many ways that could be mentioned. When you take a people who were basically a free people, who were able to worship as they please, and come and go as they please and then enslave them and take away all freedoms, how devastating do you think that is on a people? If you take a people and beat them and kill them for 400 years and mentally beat and abuse them and mentally enslave them, again how deep do you think this will affect them? It affects them so much so, that it transfers in and through the genetics and the DNA of a race of people.

The Black race has been dealing with overcoming the psychological effects of slavery since they have been physically unchained. It is a serious damaging effect that is seen in the birth of the children. As they grow it becomes more and more evident. People have been raising their children and attempting to reverse the damage done to them and their fore parents by using many methods. Some of the methods include teaching the children that they are better than the White race and to stand up and be proud of who they are. Some have taught their children hatred and racism. Some have taught their children the wrong in what happened to them as a people and not to judge, but leave it up to God to deal with, and many more methods that could be mentioned. There is something not totally correct about some of the methods mentioned, nor are all the methods totally wrong. Understand that people of the Black race have been doing the best they can with what they know and feel in order to do what they can to rid their children of the effects of slavery. They wanted their children to have a better chance at life than they had. They are teaching them to have self-worth and self- esteem about themselves and not accept that they are less than or better than.

The Nails In The Cross-A Chronicle Of Psychological Events

During slavery, look at how devastating, how deeply psychologically and subliminally affected the Black race had become. The taking away of freedom is **the first nail in the cross.** Taking people against their free will and chaining them up is saying that you are not good enough; you have no will or no rights and do not deserve anymore freedom than an animal in captivity. You become owned by some other person who did not see you as an equal or as a human being but lower than an animal.

The next nail in the cross is taking the people away from their homeland, their natural roots, their connection with the earth and the energy and spirit that occupies their homeland and feeds their soul energy and spirit with that which is natural growth and evolution. There are unseen forces that are natural to the homeland of a people and these forces are their connection to the substance of their race.

The next nail in the cross is during the taking of these people away from their home where they felt safe, loving and had something to identify with, and now that's gone and separation grows stronger, the emptiness grows larger, the lack of love is turning into fear and wonderment. The killing of many millions of these people along the way was devastating and begins to strike fear and horror in many. There were those who would rather die before they become slaves and many of them did in many, many ways. Now they lost their freedoms, their home, their love, their connection to their spiritual roots and are in the midst of experiencing untold death and horror.

The next nail in the cross comes when they reach the many locations that they were being taken. But we will focus on America. I want you to be aware that the psychological damage has begun already but is about to get deeper. The people were sent to different parts of the South of the United States and many of the families were separated. They were all in totally unfamiliar territory that carried a different kind of energy and spirit and a different kind of nurturing and spiritual force that was not conducive to their energy. They felt the energy of hatred and the smothering of life. They felt alone and confused. They were chained in groups or herds like animals and was put in barns and were feed scraps and slop and anything they, the slave owners didn't want to eat or feed their pets. They were beaten and whip like animals to keep them obedient and in line. They were set up on auction blocks and stripped completely naked, Men, Women and Children as their private parts were displayed and fondled to show good stock for breeding more animal slaves. They were beat and crucified, and castrated and cut up and you name it in the auction square to make examples out of those who tried to rebel. This had such a devastating effect mentally. They began to be afraid to stand up for themselves which was not their nature. They were a proud people who would rather die than not to stand up for themselves. Many of them did die for that reason. They begin to realize that in order to survive they had to conform to what ever the slave masters wanted. They were bought and sold like a commodity, which they were. They worked in the fields for untold hours a day while being beaten and not feed and watered.

The next nail in this great cross to bare was how they were sexually mistreated in many ways. They were made to sleep with people who they did not have love or desire for just for the sake of breeding. They were used as sex servers for the slave masters and their wives and children to fulfill their pleasures. What really hit them hard psychologically and mentally was the fact that they were forced to sleep with their own mother and fathers, daughters and sons, brothers and sisters. That was a very powerful mental and psychological effect that cut very, very deep into their heart, soul and spirit. Can you even begin to imagine what that did to them on so many levels deep and these affects have been carried from generation to generation and have revealed themselves in so many detrimental ways in people's personality and characteristics. They were in situations to where they had families in captivity and they were taken away at the whim of the slave master. They were sold at the whim of the slave master. They cared nothing about their feelings. They did not see them as families of human beings but families of animal slaves who were bred for business.

The next nail in the cross that really was very powerful and profound was the stripping them of the right to speak their native language, to talk about where they came from or any relation to their homeland. What did this do to them? It caused them to lose connection to their roots, to their language, to the connection they had to their native culture and people. They were killed if caught and that was very devastating to those who watched. They were forced to watch as they were killed, sliced up, tarred and fathered, boiled alive in oil or water, tied between two to four horses and pulled apart. Now think about the psychological damage that has been done up to this point. The babies were carried in the grips of fear and born in the grips of fear. Imagine the fear that is instilled in the unborn when the mother is forced to witness that kind of horror.

The next nail in the cross was the forcing of and the allowing of only the bible being read. They begin to give the image of a White God and Savior to them which is totally foreign to them. They were forced to accept this. As the generations were born, it was being literally beaten and bred into them. The teachings of the bible that were given to the Black people served to make them mentally retarded. It served to instill fear, passivity and obedience to that which was supposed to be superior. They lost all sight of self-worth and dignity. They were taught out of their heritage and out of their rightful mind. They were reduced to nothing but less than animals and everything Good, Pure, Righteous and Godly was White skinned. As a Black people, they had nothing to look up to but pain, suffering, death, slavery, and not ever being good enough for anything but serving the interest of the White race. The Black race was saturated with many psychological detriments.

Psychological Detriments By Association

These detriments will include things that will be mentioned here but not limited to these things, such as relating everything Black to bad and everything White to good. Let's take a look at some examples. Look at how subtle and how outright things were set in motion to keep Black people psychologically damaged. This was very well thought about and implemented long before the physical releasing of slavery. The intention was to keep them slaves and chained but with more space to move around in. Look at the references to things like: The good guys wear white and the bad guys wear black and it was projected in television, films, plays and books. Angel food cake is white and devils food cake is black. The angels are pure and white and the angel that is bad is the angel of death or the angel of the devil. Look at what so many films have projected for so long, always showing the Black person as the house nigger, slave or servant. Even now with the films, when it is a cast of predominantly Black people it is called a Black movie. When it is a cast of dominantly White people it is called a movie. All this still continues to promote separation among humanity. The daylight is safe, but in the black or dark of night, bad things happen or the bogey men come in the dark etc. etc. etc. At weddings you wear white but at funerals and death all wear black. I can go on and on with examples of these references that are subliminally damaging. Look around you and you can see mountains of these examples that you never paid any attention to before. Look at his-story or what is called history.

Damage Done Through His-Story (History)

What place does Black people have in history compared to the great White culture? How damaging is it to a young Black child to grow up and be taught Black history by a White person who is teaching about Black slavery. That seems to be the biggest story in Black history and made out for the most part to be the only story. His-story shows that all the great minds and Spiritual Avatars in history were all White Skinned People. Jesus, Moses, Mother Mary, Cleopatra, the Pharaohs, Isis, and an enormous amount of great historical figures were all represented as being White Beings. What does the Black child have to look up to? Everything White is superior and all else is inferior, especially the Black. This has literally destroyed the minds of the Black child who grows up at a disadvantage in psyche, mind, inner feeling, etc. Some are blessed enough to not be affected by it to a point to where it is detrimental to them. Yet many run into these invisible racial blocks that come with having black skin. Some Whites are even unaware of how they act toward Black people because it is inbreed in them, and therefore, they are acting normal as far as they know and they are not able to see what they are doing. Yet, Black people do recognize these actions because they are very sensitive to them. And there are so many other considerations, like having that token Black involved so it will look right. It is alright to have 100 Whites and 1 Black because that makes it alright. It doesn't make it alright. None of it makes it alright. As humanity, we must begin to break down these barriers of separation by color and differences.

We have to come together as a people, as a human family, as the Children of the Creator to tear down these lies and deceitful means and judgments that are prevalent in our society. These racial stigmas are not healthy for anyone, not only the Black people. Black people are judged by so many criteria. When many successful Blacks are looked at, they are still seen as that ghetto nigger who is doing well or got lucky. Many people still say that all Blacks have that ghetto mentality and are about sex, drugs and irresponsible actions and so forth. They are full of crime and are thieves and cannot be trusted and you name it. You know how the story goes. This is changing now to a degree and it will get bigger as time goes on but it is not changing quickly enough. When people start to accept people as people then things will change. What is going to help this change much more quickly is the fact that so many spiritual beings are entering the Earth.

The Youth Will Affect Change

Many of the youth of all cultures such as Asian, Hispanic, Latino and especially the White youth are embracing the Black culture even though they are embracing only one aspect of it. Most of what they are embracing is the hip hop/rap culture, dress and mannerisms. There is a whole lot more to Black culture than that but yet, this is how Blacks are basically viewed This is a beginning to a greater understanding of Blacks and there true heritage. You'll find that the Black influence is everywhere. Even many of the adult Whites are not so afraid to speak about Blacks and use many of the black terms and music. The young White youth are trying to say to the world that there is nothing wrong with Blacks. We love what they are and what they are doing. We can vibe with that, we can hang with that and we can embrace that. We feel no prejudice toward them. In fact, we admire a lot of things about them. They think it is cool to be Black.

The damage that has been psychologically done to Whites, are now starting to reveal itself even more through their children. Many of them have this guilt about being White and want to show that they are not like their parents or grandparents or forefathers and mothers. They are mentally disturbed by a lot of this racial stigma and the treating of Blacks. One thing that is not realized is that many of these White youth may have been Black in another life and they carry that in their DNA and all that goes with it. Why did they come back in White skin? Well, maybe because they see it to their advantage to do that to better break down this separation by color.

The youth population of the White race are the biggest buyers of Black music and clothes of anyone. In fact, There are many Whites who are rapping and sounding like Black hip hop artist as well as Black R&B singers. I really do not like the separation of using the term Black music because when it is referring to that which is music made by White people is not called White music it is just music.

They are embracing the Black culture as their own and the parents cannot stop them. Many Whites are working so diligently to help Black people because they feel guilt. They feel better about themselves when they can say that they do this and that for Black people, when they can say that I'm not prejudice, I have Black friends, etc. Now, I am not saying this is the case with all White people but it is with many of them. The White race is opening up to levels of compassion. They're opening up to levels of evolution. They're opening up to levels of expansion that needed to happen on the Earth that had to happen on the Earth and let us say, that many of these are some of what you call the new children holding the new energies. The new energies are energies of unity. It is a certain energy of love, and I am not saying it is only the White race but many within the White race are reversing what you might call the genetics of politics, the genetics of separation. They have come in for that purpose. They are opening up to unity, to the consciousness of unity that they have felt perhaps for a long time. Maybe even their parents felt something was really wrong but were afraid to get involved because maybe it would alienate them from their own race. Some have gotten involved and many aren't. So the youth are saying "I don't want to be part of it, I want to be a part of mending this." So many of the new children have come in through that line of evolution.

Let's consider the psychic children in Japan. And also consider the aids babies that will not get sick and have reversed the illness. In many areas all races are bringing through these children who hold new genetics. Now, let us look at it as DNA and let's look at my question when I said that I wanted to unblock memory, cellular memory. This is the time for the restoration of what you would call the ten lost children, the ten lost strands or strings of the DNA, opening up higher brain consciousness, higher alertness and awareness. There not missing, they are in the DNA, there just not on line, they need reconnection. Many of the children today are born with this connection.

The Black White Thing

So the point I want to make here is that both Black and White are affected by this Black/ White thing that goes on. It seems that everything is based around Black and White. Decisions, Laws, Opinions, etc., are based around this Black/ White issue. In fact, there have been certain laws passed specifically geared toward the Black race. It is true! Everyone knows it! What is it that brings so much fear of Black people that certain people will go to any lengths to keep them completely smothered? I want you to understand that none of this that I speak of here is done to separate or to cause guilt. There is no dislike or racism involved in the writing of these words of truth at all. It is only truth, unconditional love and light with the desire to unite all people. We must first begin with the truth and deal with this sensitive issue of Black and White. Why are people so sensitive about this? Why do people feel so uneasy about this? It is the affects of severe mental and psychological damage. As a human race, as a people, let us all unite to bring together this separation for the greater good of humanity and the greater good of the plan of the Spiritual Hierarchy.

Oprah Winfrey- A courageous Human Being

I want to make mention here of Oprah Winfrey. She did a show that was very powerful and very revealing about how people are really affected by color and differences. This is a verification of what we have been saying here about separation and how psychologically affected people are without even knowing it. Oprah did a show that involved her audience without their awareness that was to show how racism exists in people even if they are not aware of it. She separated the audience by what were really very insignificant differences such as eye color, hair color, and skin complexion. Certain ones were treated differently from others according to the difference that any given group had from the other. They were given more attention and told things that made them feel superior. It was amazing to see how their attitudes changed toward the other people and how they actually believed that they were better, because of those minor differences.

At the end of the show, Oprah revealed to her studio audience that they had been unknowing participants of an experiment to show that racism and prejudice still exists even though many say that they are not. The participants seemed to easily buy into what was happening and not one stood up and questioned why they were being treated differently from others. Oprah did something that was very important in breaking down the barrier that exists, that is unseen but yet, it is there. What she did during that show took insight and courage and a lot of heart. It opened up a lot of eyes that day, not only within the audience but in the viewers as well. People do not know that Oprah Winfrey has a mission that transcends the color lines and that is of a great humanitarian nature. She has so much more to do than people know and she is an Ambassador of the light for the Spiritual Hierarchy and is one who is in tune with the one known as the Heart Master. I will not go into details about what I know without her permission and maybe someday I will get to speak to her at length about her future role with humanity. I want to thank her dearly for the many great services she provides to humanity through her show and the best is yet to come. She provides a service to people all over the world through her show which has profound affects on many people and helped to positively change their lives. The Spiritual Hierarchy is pleased with her work. Thank You, Oprah, very much with great love, oneness and blessings to you from me, the author, and all of those here in the Spiritual Dimensions.

Chapter 5
The Great Divine Experiment

In this chapter, we will take a look at the great Divine plan that was implemented so, so long ago. It is a plan that was very masterfully thought out. Yet it was an experiment to see if it could work. The human race has no idea the depths of what this entire plan involved. It involved other races of Extraterrestrial origin and many, many of the Masters and Angels to participate in this great experiment. It was a very immaculately laid plan that would involve about ten major planets all with different species. It was to be the most profound thing ever done to date in creation. Some of what you are about to read may not be understood by many and it will take a very open mind spiritually, and the moving away from the human analytical mind. It cannot be reasoned with rational thought or thinking. You can't fathom what is going on with your limited reasoning, linear, third dimensional mind.

So, we say to you to be open and prepare yourself. It is very difficult to bring certain information to humanity because of the conditionings and the learning's of humanity. There is another difficulty that involves the sequencing of time and knowledge to that of the level of the Earth's timing and the sequencing of knowledge. It is difficult to explain why certain knowledge is not allowed or open to humanity, because much of what we learned in school, family and in history is not exactly accurate. It is very inaccurate from another level of time knowledge and sequencing, particularly that of another planet, where the events of Earth may have been played out differently or sequenced differently. There is a great distortion on Earth because of so many imbalances that happened on the planet. It is being rectified now but much work still needs to be done.

I will share with you what the Master D.K. had to say about time and the sequencing of knowledge. I ask you to take your time and follow slowly and carefully what is being said. And remember to be careful about so much rationalization about what is being said. Open your heart and mind and ask for the guidance of your Higher Self.

A Talk With D.K.

Blessings and greetings to you, beloved one, I am D. K. and I have come to assist with the continuation of some of the questions that you have asked in regards to the study that you have now been engaged in for a little while. I ask that you stop for a moment and bring yourself, into a depth in the heart. And I ask that you balance yourself, that you ground yourself that you enter into the depth of the sanctuary that has been revealed to you many times. A way in which to bring an opening into the heart, a way in which to apply oneself, protect oneself and sit to hear that which is behind words. For I wish to bring to you a little bit of information this day that might assist you in understanding the nature of questions and the nature of answers. And of course, I will also bring some light to bare on some of your questions but not all of them will be answered in the ways in which you would like, and I will tell you why. Certain knowledge and understandings in and around and on Earth go a little bit with the territory of the Earth, you might say. In other words, there is a way in which to measure time on Earth. The way that time is measured on the Earth is not measured the same in other worlds. I would like you to open up the windows of the mind for a moment. Open up to the possibility of having your mind blown as they would say on the Earth. Could it be that in your galaxy there could be 90,000 or so, give or take a little here a little there, planets with life? I would like for you to understand that there are many planets with life in this galaxy very, very many. But I also would like for you to understand that there are different doctrines and different ways of looking at things and different ways of measuring time. So in one sense is time real?

I want you to understand that the volume of knowledge and information that is associated with the Planet Earth are a little bit restricted and a little bit withheld. If you took them and compared them to that which is known in other existences you will find that they don't correspond. In so it is not quite so easy to answer some of the questions, for some of that knowledge is not held available. Is it not reachable? Of course it is, but some of it is actually archived, is actually a little hidden, is actually not quite completely appropriate to bring out in this way, and you might say why? I might say there are a lot of planets in the Galaxy and many in the Solar System and many in the Universe and there is a certain different set of parameters and principles that goes along with each you might say. And it's not exactly accurate to pin it down to an Earth understanding as you would want to think. The mind of someone on Earth looks at things and say, 'well there is a right answer and there is a wrong answer.' It looks at things as right and wrong and greater than and less than and all of that. This has been forced and taught upon all of you. And it is a way of seeing things and measuring them and understanding them. The entire study of Earth life is very fascinating and very illuminating to many in Higher Realms and Worlds that have never experienced anything quite like it. So please be aware that it is quite unique on the Earth.

Time, knowledge and sequencing.

Please also be aware that many things happened in what you would call your history and that many things are repeated and they are recorded in quite a different way, so that certain things came back, and back, and back again in different time frames. Yet, they were recorded on Earth in a certain sequence that wasn't exactly the way it was. The difference in sequencing are honored and held within the other worlds. Let us say that certain races inhabited the planet Earth, within the great Divine plan, of all the Divine plans, all uniting and existing in unity and yet not in unity of time, because it isn't really like that. If I were to explain to you what time is I couldn't because the channel could not really conceive of it in language, although the channel is beginning to open up to possibilities and potentialities that time is nothing like what it is called and experienced on the Earth. In other words, side effects of time are considered within the definition of time and time is simply energy. It is different in all energetic patterns, therefore, it isn't a constant. Because of that, it is not so easy to bring information that has a certain sequencing and a certain time, to the Earth while the mental bodies on the Earth, and this isn't a criticism, are not quite opened to the total understanding of the concept of time or the experience of time. All these things are going to shift very soon. Therefore, when this attempt is made to sequence something for you, it is almost as if there are overlays and certain things get hidden in the process. Please try to understand, that all you want to know and need to know will be brought to you in the rightness of time. And often the Masters are hated, very much disliked for saying these sorts of things. People say, "I want to know now, I have a right to know now" and yet this knowledge does not fall easily in a stack upon the table. In fact, what will free you up probably the most rather than the answers to the questions, is the energy of this explanation of how all the different energies, although connected and united, for all is energy and all is united, how all of it has a different level of things, so that one planet and another planet, although connected will see things in quite a different way.

What We have Been taught on Earth is not accurate

Alright, so some knowledge is hidden. It is not meant to be placed in Earth sentences and given out. Some of it is not yet revealable because it tends to be based upon a shuffling of the way that things are categorized and understood on Earth. Those things most cherished, and we said this before, those ideals most held to, those belief systems most adhered to, are not exactly the way things are. And yet, it is not exactly the time to try to put every thing into a sequence, which is a little bit of the confusion and the confrontation of some of the nature of some of these questions. Probably the greatest gift of this hour is, if your mind can begin to bring in a ray of light that would tell you to keep going and going and going in the way that you are going and be ready to begin to trace back and to know that almost all of what you have been taught in school, in family, in the history of Earth is not the history, it is not the story that is accurate. Many, many holes are still there, where truth has fallen through.

Within the humanity on Earth, all of you, you, you, and you hold the key, a key that is so precious and so priceless and so important to the whole of the galaxies, all of those 90,000 planets with life in this galaxy, all those aspects that see more, know more have different qualities and different qualities of time, that they experience, are still in awe of you. Within the seed that you carry, the light with the soul, the spark of divinity that spirit within, deep, deep, deep individuation has brought you to where you end up being the key holder, the key itself to a certain very important unity process, gifting glory so that all of those Extra-terrestrials, Angels and Light Beings and many, many, many Masters are wanting the completion on Earth to take place and with it your entire system within systems, for all is connected is going to go up another level.

So little bits will stream in little openings, little doors and little tributaries carry the water. So I guarantee you that at one time you will most likely go up in a space ship and you will be shown many things that can be revealed to you out of the context that is Earth. But the preparation is to simply open the mind and open the heart and know that things are not at all as they have been taught to you in any shape, way or form. Things are very, very much different than has been revealed to the population on Earth. So in one sense you can say that the Earth is the hope of the Galaxy, the hope of the Universe, the hope of the Solar System, it is the hope of Earth it is the hope of God. Why? Because all are connected and if you go into and meditate on the connectivity of everything, you will almost see a little bit of the complexity of trying to sort out all of these things and how they came to be. They do exist. But there are versions of the truth that are very different and they are all present. The Earth versions of the truth have lots of holes, lots of crevices in them. Doesn't mean that you can judge the Earth or would want to judge the Earth, or think that something is wrong with humans, because I just told you that something is so right with humanity.

Divisions and Individuations

Humanity was strong enough to go into deep, deep division, deep, deep individuation only to be strong; still enough to carry that spark back into unity without all those truths and all this knowledge hidden and open. And because of that you will come back to the hidden knowledge, the other knowledge and everything will come into a bright explosion. But in the meantime, in this one moment, it is not going to be so easy. It would be for you to decide if you want to explore any of this further or not. As the channel has told you that certain things are going to come through you, not through the channel, because it is meant that you bring them through. And also, some of it has to do with the timing. There is some information that is put on tablets, out in books, put on scrolls, ancient information. And this knowledge needs to come, be discovered and be brought forth and not hindered by governments, by agendas, by controllers but brought out and shared with the public of Earth. This needs to happen and it is one of the things that we are setting up, that many are setting up. There is other knowledge that can never be put in words, can never be printed on stone and will not be put into scrolls hidden under pyramids or the sphinx.

Author's Comments:

I want to take a moment and further explain the above statement by D.K. The experiment that was the divine plan was based on the human species going into this with a challenge that was nearly impossible from the start. The plan was to take the human species into very deep division and very deep individuation, a very deep disunity. Then they had to some how work through all this and still maintain enough strength to find their way back into unity without the advantage of knowing and having the necessary truths and not having access to the knowledge that was hidden. We came here and forgot. It was done to the humans purposefully. They, the creators of this Divine plan, wanted to know what it would take to come here basically blind, with no direction or no awareness of the truth and knowledge, coming into diversity and disunity and find our way back to oneness. They wanted to know if it could be done, can the humans of this Earth do it. They had to come back into knowledge and hidden knowledge and find out what had to be done to accomplish this mission. Also note that one couldn't even begin to come into certain knowledge unless the timing was right. There is plenty of knowledge that is available that needs to come forward to all humanity so they can evolve to a much higher state of being. But it has to come at a time to when it will be free enough to share with all humanity without the interference of those who wish to control. Also understand that there is knowledge that can never be written about or put in words, because it would be impossible to transfer this into words. It has to be understood in a different way as explained in our book on the Mushaba Force. It will take means that are non physical. This experiment is very interesting because of the great magnitude of what it will accomplish. We will go into that a little later. Let us return to D.K.

<u>Separation Is No One's Fault</u>

Upon learning of separation, upon learning the game of separation, it is no one's fault. The game of separation was a game that was downloaded into the consciousness, because it had something to do with the Divine plan of going from individuation and back into wholeness, and going from disunity, back into unity, going from separation into group consciousness. Its part of what took place as an experiment with out a fault, and the separation of greater than and lesser than, evil and good, bigger and better, and stronger and weaker, all of that comes from the Earth not from the Heavens. They don't look at things within Hierarchy, They don't look at things so much in the greater and lesser than, Oh no! They don't look through the separation lens. When imbalance comes into a person, that person will act and react, think and feel, within a loss of balance. Then, they might wish to take into them something to balance them, so they might take it from someone else. They might feel they need to bolster up something. So many things have happened but the important part is that it is all a stage, a drama, an event. Many events have taken place and now it is the time of reunification. Maybe certain tribes had certain Extra-Terrestrial origins that were slightly different and they acted slightly different and looked slightly different. If you're going to play the game of separation then you are going to look through the eyes that see separation.

You have forgotten certain things, within the plan all along. Because it was never the plan that the races would be seeded upon the Earth in full memory of why they came, what they're doing, what their heritage is and all their past life times and what planet they were from. Because, then the game plan would have been totally different. So they came as amnesiacs, as if with amnesia, and that is why I and others bow down to all of you who are willing to play this game, to bring the knowledge, different knowledge into the libraries of God. And in the process of playing the game, they have forgotten much of the other knowledge that others have, and yet, all will be brought back to you. So, let us say that even the struggle, obviously giving up your heritage, giving up your memory, choosing to volunteer to go into the experiment on Earth, the reality of Earth life, to go into a lowered bit of consciousness and so forth, obviously it would be a little bit of a struggle. What are they going to do with struggle? How are they going to act with struggle? Many things were looked at, many things were learned about, and whether you realize it or not, there are also worlds that are not even as advanced as yours.

But understand that generally, in an evolved world, spirituality and love go hand and hand with technology. When they do not, the planet usually blows itself up and that has happened. When things get a little bit forgotten then they get a little bit almost made up. When the truth is missing, then untruths and half truths and partial truths come into being. Then translations of truth can get very muddy and they can cause more of a struggle. Let us let us say that the struggle is ending, let us say that the acceleration is on the upgrade, the unification is on the upgrade.

Laws Within Higher Realms

There are laws within higher realms that certain things need to be told in a different way, as in mental telepathy, in hidden ways, not in language and not in words. So these things will also be gifts, that you will uncover and unveil, but it won't be in language. Perhaps it will be in the language of Light. Please know, that older than any language in words, is the language of vibration, the language of geometry, the language of life and tone, motion and vibration. All of this wants to be downloaded onto the Earth and everything is setting up in order to receive all that, in due time.

Earth's Out Post And Pre- History

You need to know, that in the history of Earth, there is a great deal of history that took place as pre-history that is not in any history book, not any. Some of this information is coming in from the inside to the outside, through channels, through those who have awakened and through those who sought this out. Some are discovering that Extra- terrestrials are responsible for all the races on the Earth not just the Black race. Extra-terrestrials have had diverse outposts on Earth since the beginning of what you call time. Many of these outposts were present, many of them died out, many of the occupants went back to where they came from, many of them came back, and there has been a back and a forth and a back and a forth, since the beginning on the Earth, since the seeding of life on the Earth. There were also outposts of ET's and humans in hybrid, all of this you know already. Many different races came from your Solar System and others came from other Solar Systems. Many came from what is the called the Sunsnake System. Many came from very far away, many places were set up, many meeting places were honored and many came to the Earth. Many introduced a species from here and a species from there and it is very complex. Many came and took others with them and went somewhere and came back again. So your answer is not so simplistic and the lines cannot be drawn so easily. There have been many mixes. Many came back when things had changed. Many different sorts of life have been upon the Earth at certain times, when life was large and times when it was small. Many came into the outposts and many left and came back a second time in a different way.

Contribution To The Races Of Earth

Many of the species were begun, were started, not evolving from apes as many have been told, not the survival of the fittest, but with the introduction of shared DNA. It is knowledge that ten major species from ten major planets went into the mixing, from the different planetary worlds, to come into the different qualities on the Earth. Please know that on Earth, there is diversity on earth that is nowhere else. In many worlds, there might be one, maybe there are two, sorts of offerings of life. Maybe there is one race, one language, one vibrational language. Maybe, there are a few animal lives, certain species of plant life streams. In many worlds, there is a humanoid aspect and maybe a reptilian aspect. In some worlds there is a little bit of two very different races, very different, not human races of different color and decent, but very different. And, in some, there is a uniformity, very much of a one.

So the experiment on the earth was very different and very purposeful and very diverse. There is a quality that was introduced to that which you would call the Japanese, the Chinese, the Eskimo population, the American Indians, the Indians from India, the Africans, the darker Africans a lot of the tall ones and the Arabic people. Then there is the lighter more northern European sort of Nordic White pale races that came from other worlds. Grecian people and Spanish people, all of them mixed up, even more mixed up and interbred than now. They were coming from many worlds. Now, some of those worlds are very different than they were at that time and some of those worlds are more similar. So you could say, "wouldn't it be wonderful if all the Japanese people could go back to their Japanese planet." Maybe they would like it, maybe they wouldn't. Maybe they would feel at home, maybe they wouldn't, things change. The White race came from certain planets where all pale skin people came from, with blonde hair, maybe bluish eyes, maybe they look a little bit like the ones now, and maybe they looked a bit different. Lots of mixing and matching took place.

Now, you might say, "why don't you tell me what those ten planets are and tell me which one goes with which." I don't have the authority to do that, and I don't have the go ahead, and the green light to do that. Let us say that as things exist right now, there were twelve planets and each thought that they were one of the ten? Perhaps there are fifty planets and each thought that they were one of the ten. Are there really a ten? In what time? In what sequence? And in what way? Is it pure or is it mixed in? So it isn't so easy to give the name of each of the planets, the one that birthed the White race, the one that birthed the African race and the truth is, all of that, you may find one day in a history book, on another planet in an evolved sort of situation, and it would give you some information.

What you need to know right now, is what I'm telling you, which will open your heart and open your mind. The other information, were you to have it, what would you do with it? But the information that I give you now will open the mind and open the heart, rather than categorizing and rather than simply giving an explanation. Are there libraries yes. It would be almost like stepping on someone's foot, if one planet was left out in my download to you of what the ten were? What if there were two planets contributing and what if it seems as if most of the goodies came from one planet, but one other planet felt like it had a lot to offer? So simply for me not to exclude, not to separate, it isn't appropriate right now and the channel will not bring that information through, of just which planets exactly, contributed. But simply know that many species went into the seeding of the Earth for a purpose of diversity, coming into unity, for a purpose of individuation, compassion, understanding, and forgiveness amidst very strong inherent differences.

Can You Trust The Differences

Now some people say, because they want everyone to get along they say everyone's the same. They all have the same DNA do they not? They're all the same so why can't they all get along? The truth is, they are all the same, all is one but there are differences. There are some very tall tribes in Africa, the people are very, very tall and there are some planets in the galaxy where many grow to a very tall height. It didn't just happen when they got to Africa and were born through the passage of the seeds. There was a quality in those original races to be tall. There are some Extraterrestrial races that are quite short, 4 ft. tall, quite different. So please know that it is diversity, and it is heritage, and yet the important thing is, that within all of it, there is unity, there is cohesion, there is compassion.

There is no need to dislike or distrust those who are different. In fact, that is the major lesson of all of this, because when the Extraterrestrials come to make contact with you and the others, if they do not look like you, then it will be very interesting how they will be received. What if they look very different? What if they look sort of different? In fact, there are many, many, many differences in the local universe. Compassion is the most important thing. There is a grand unity and a scale of unity unheard of, a love unheard of, and a compassion unheard of on Earth.

Group Consciousness is God

Please know that it isn't always the particulars, but the understanding, that will set you free. This group consciousness is where everything is going. Group consciousness is God, Group consciousness is Creator. Everything is actually joined and united. With everything joined and united, you can meditate for one year upon those words alone, and set yourself free, if you went into the quality of what that is. So, there's much overlap. Individuation is the keynote of the game of separation and karma that took place on the Earth, but only to go from individuation back into group consciousness, still holding the individuation but going into cosmic consciousness and thereby lifting everything into a higher level. There are beings who don't know anything about individuation. They live only in group consciousness.

Author's Comments:

It is said and understood by many that all this is heading back to where it came, which is group consciousness. There will be a major difference that was not here before. The Creator learns and expands and gets larger by sending out the many aspects of itself to learn and to explore and to bring back that which it has learned. So, the great game was played. The great game was set into motion, the great game of separation and karma and the playing field for this magnificent game were to be the Earth. The main rule, or the keynote rule, was to play in individuation and this made it so much more challenging and difficult to accomplish. What is, in a sense, the penalty for not uncovering the truth of the game? Is it that you cannot move out of the game? How was one to successfully play the game when they are in separation, division, and individuation? When the rules in a sense were broken or not followed, the penalty was to come back and try again. This rule was called karma. Karma allowed one to return again and again to play the game, to finally get it right.

So what had to be done was to start the game with separation, disunity, individuation, karma, and forgetfulness of what you are playing and why you are playing. Then you some how had to remember that you forgot that you were playing a game and that you forgot why you were playing the game. Then you had to begin to work on coming into a oneness and balance with all the diversity that you experienced. You had to come into unity and not hold on to the losing team, which was separation. Now the trick was that you had to come into unity, oneness and remembrance, as well, as make tracks back to where the game started which was from the higher dimensions. You had to find your way back to group consciousness, realizing that it is all connected and unified and the illusion that you played with, was what kept you from winning all along. The final trick was to return to group consciousness in unity and oneness and still maintain your individuation, but yet be one.

When you do that you score big points by seeing all things lift up to a higher level. It is being watched by many beings from many different planets, because they have no idea what it is to be in disunity and separation and have an individuation, let alone to go through all that, return to group consciousness and maintain your individuation and oneness. They have no idea what it is like or to be outside of group consciousness.

So, the Earth Human had a rare opportunity to experience something that is quite wondrous and unique in Creation, something that has never been done before. What a rich experience and opportunity this is. So, it has to be recognized that this is something that the Creator wanted to see the outcome of and experience the outcome through each of the points of views of each aspect of Himself/Herself that It sent out from Itself. This is a very deep thing that is happening on Earth. There are many who could not do it and didn't want to take the chance. But you are doing it and the rewards are quite wondrous to say the least. Lets continue with D. k.

See The S In Everyone

Know that the main freedom will be when you begin to connect the dots yourself within all of this language and simply begin to see that you are not Black nor White, nor African or American on Earth, that you are a God being, literally wearing many faces. And that everyone that comes before you has no face, no history, no anything. They have the face of **Spirit.** They have a big **S** over themselves. When you see your mother, **S.** When you see your father, **S.** When you see the president of the United States, it's a big **S.** You see everyone on the street, its **Spirit**, and each one has something about Spirit to reveal to you for all are Spirit. No matter what they say, no matter how they say it, what they look like, how they look, their age, their color, their religion, their creed, all of these differences are set within the similarity of oneness. And when this happens, there can be no judgment. The lion not only lies down with the lamb, but protects the lamb and everything smaller and everything larger. There is a code of life which has to do with the substance that all life has, whether it is dark or light in its acquaintance. Whether it's on the side of the light or the side of the dark, Love is in all, no matter what, and this is what needs to come out, absolutely.

Can The Earth Hold The Balance

Earth is not in a state of balance, but recently came into the possibility of holding enough balance, so that the Divine plan can actually complete itself. Many things set Earth out of balance, many histories, that which you would call asteroids, that which you would call planets. Earth once had two moons and the Earth had more balance. Two is a balance, one side and the other holding something up, masculine and feminine. Your Universe is based on this kind of polarity consciousness all the way through. It isn't seen as evil or good, it is seen as balance. Many things happened in your Solar System. Many planets that once were there are not there now and some caused many explosions. Think of the imbalances that take place. In Afghanistan, in all the places where destruction and war exist. I want you to think of Lemuria and Atlantis and the sinking of those continents and all the imbalances in thought for all is thought and emotion for all is feeling and it all went forth to create greater and greater unbalance. Many survivors from those places were moved around, were carried off, lifted off by ET's, by Angels, in many ways lifted off and evacuated and brought to bare in a different part upon the Earth. In Egypt many of those survived and they became the ones you would know as the Pharaohs.

The Pharaohs

And I will tell you this, all Pharaohs, all those who go under the heading of Pharaohs, were a mixture of Extra-terrestrial and human. And when the time came that the E.T's would leave, the humans would be more or less on their own and they were used as a slave race. Slavery was in Egypt with the Pharaohs. And then it became apparent, that there were many so called Pharaohs who had then evacuated from the planet leaving what you would call lesser Pharaohs, what you would call lesser leaders. What do I mean by that? More Human, less Extra-terrestrial, and not having, the power of Gods and Goddesses. The Pharaohs were seen as Gods, they were seen as Goddesses. Why? Because they had the higher ET blood lines. So I would say to you that this one that you speak of, Pharaoh Kafre, I would say yes, that this one had something to do with, the building of pyramids, but not only this one but this ones progeny, what you would call children.

The Sphinx

I want you to know the significance of the head of the sphinx that is called the lion. I want you to understand that the lion is a very important symbol, very important, but I cannot tell you how or why it is so important at this time. It is almost like a hand is coming over my mouth or the mouth of the channel. Bare in mind, over the next 2-3 years, you will most likely discover what the importance of the lion is. There are many who consider that the Pharaoh, the Pharaoh's likeness was exhibited in the sphinx. The Pharaoh, who is associated with having his tomb, be the second pyramid.

Please know that the combination of human and lion is very significant in its Extra-terrestrial origins. Please also know that the time line that is given by you, and by probably many texts, isn't exactly as it should be written and this goes back to our entrance into the session when we were talking about time and how it is perceived in entirely different ways. Without there being a right and a wrong, but seen in many, many ways there is what is called loops of time that are completely unknown within human consciousness. So I would say to you. This one, the Pharaoh of which you speak, had very strong and deep Extra- terrestrial ties and knowledge.

Clearing Of Cellular Memory

Note: "The clearing of cellular memory can help one to access the truth of the knowledge that was forgotten. So I thought to include a little bit of information on this, so who ever you choose to help you with this clearing, be very sure that they really know what they are doing."

D.K.

You have asked, how can I clear cellular memory? How can I clear out blocks? I would say that this is already happening. If you want to work on it in a very forceful way, in a very wonderful way, find someone to do some DNA work. But realize that everything has a consciousness and you can speak to matter, you can speak to the cells and you can help them to let go of those things that they carry in their deep libraries, that are for the most part, not even true, not even accurate, or a mixture. There is a little bit of truth in all the religions, in all of the philosophies, not the whole truth and nothing but the truth but in many things there is a little bit. Clear out the cellular libraries and then find some way in which to literally dialog with those parts of you, so that you treat matter in a Divine way. And talk to it as if it has intelligence, because it does.

Please know the bodies are changing extremely, in extreme ways. The skin is the largest organ; there are many skin changes, many DNA changes, many cellular changes, charkas changes, acupuncture point changes, many changes, some you have heard of, some you have not heard of. Where ever there is a weakness in a particular body, there will be a little bit of a challenge. So there is no reason to think that just because you are spiritual, and doing all the work, that you will have no challenges to the body. For many are having many challenges in the body and many shifts and challenges in the skin denote changes within the system of the body. Sometimes they take a little time but it is temporary.

Make sure that you are eating what you want to eat, what you feel drawn to eat and not following some procedure that worked at a different time. Make sure you drink a lot of water to wash out the toxins because they need to be washed out to keep the lymph system open.

Blessings to you beloved one. Sit in the sanctuary of heart now as I touch your heart and send you love. Blessings upon you, now and in the intensity of this transition as you birth the Christ seed in a deeper way, as you come to know the deep knowledge held within you. You are your self knowledge, you are your self ecstasy, you are your self leader and within the consciousness of a larger and larger group, as many circles fitting within the others, and in one way there is no such thing as alone. Amen

Chapter 6
__Ascended Master Afra Speaks__

__Ascended Master Afra__

I am Afra an Ascended Master that is working with Sananda and I come from many places on the continent. I work with many peoples and to understand what our thinking is you must go into the drumming, you must go into the pulse, you must go into the rhythm, you must be able to speak to the Earth, you must think like you are in the Native area. We are very tied into the Spirit world, we are very tied into the ancient times, and we are very tied into the Mother Planet. I, Afra, have been involved with the creative spiritual life of the African native peoples and I have been providing guidance and wisdom for them to become aware of their connections to the Earth, and to their connections to the Primordial Force. The Primordial Force is basically a very powerful, energetic and life giving force that is not a destructive force. It is not a force to be afraid of, but it is a force that is transcending the consciousness. It is a force that is transcending into a state of trance in which you can go into other realms and you can meet your Father and Mother Spirits, and you can go to other planets.

It is true that our peoples did not have the sophisticated understanding of the scientific world. We did not have the sophisticated understanding of the different planets. We knew of the different species, we knew of the different Beings but we did not understand, the way the people do today about the different Galaxies and the different Solar

Systems and the different Planets and those places in the Universe. We did understand that there were different peoples. We did understand that they came from places beyond where our native lands were. And because of this we were very sophisticated in our knowledge and very sophisticated in our communications.

Our Mission

Our mission was to bring forth this creative energy and to assist in the development of the consciousness of man and we did do that. We did assist in bringing the human species beyond the animal thinking planet world, into a conscious being, into a Being that was walking in a state that was more of what you would call, human, more God like, more like a thinking conscious Being. We did this through a force. The force, as you know it, in your current technology, is called the Mushaba Force. It was a creative force and it was a force of consciousness, it was a force of light, it was a force of awareness, For we knew that in order for Beings to evolve into consciousness, they must come into an awareness of Self. They must be able to bring down the Universal Mind into the conscious mind of the Being on the planet. You know that the mind itself does not exist in this reality.

What you are seeing of people's mind is the manifestation of their mind, of their, shall we say, thoughts that come from another Realm. Just like your body is manifested but the core soul connection comes from another realm. And we were able to instill an awareness enough to help the species go to a higher plane, to go to a higher state of consciousness. And now, you, my friend, who ask, What is the next role for the Mushaba Energy?

The Activation Of Native Thinking

The Mushaba Energy is a creative force energy that is able to activate native thinking. Native thinking means love of the Earth, Native thinking means protecting the Earth, Native thinking means protecting the customs that helps one to connect with the Spiritual forces beyond nature and beyond the visible. It means that there must be brought forth an awareness of the role that the Black people played in the development of the world, in the development of the species. Because you and I both know that if the Black people did not take this mission, then the Beings that you know now as the human beings, Mankind, the Earth Beings, would not have evolved. Because they took the first step, they took the first energy and moved it forward so that we could bring forth the species. This is a wonderful contribution.

But now there is a necessity to unite all native species, to unite all natives, whether it be the Native Americans, whether it be the minds of the Natives of the Australia peninsula and the Black peoples, because all of the Natives now are needed to reactivate the Earth, to reactivate the consciousness of the Earth Beings so that they can help to heal the planet, so they can help to bring forth the 5th dimensional light and bring forth the Earth harmony.

The Destruction of Africa

We are very concerned now about the destruction of the African continent and we are very concerned about the destruction of the Black peoples throughout the Earth, but even more so, on the continent of Africa. There is a great decimation of the population and it is a great tragedy far beyond even what is being told now and this is being neglected, this is being overlooked as a major catastrophe. But when the time comes and people will look, and they will see that the world cannot survive without the Africans. The world cannot survive without African energy because the African energy is the basis, it is the Father Energy, it is the Mother Energy, and it is the core, the Soul of the Beings of the Earth that keeps people connected. With the loss of that connection, more chaos would follow. I, Afra, am sending you blessings and we will send a beam of golden light into the continent of Africa so that she can be reborn.

The Evolution of Human Kind

There is a time for the rebirth of Africa, and perhaps, you can take part of this mission upon yourself. The rebirth includes not only the healings of the disease of the Black people there but also a renewal and appreciation on this planet so that the planet becomes aware of the role that the Blacks and the Africans played in the development of the civilized world, the development of human kind and the role of the evolution. Because we know, as you know that there is now at this moment, a very important step in evolution. There is an important evolutionary step that must be taken to bring mankind to the next level.

Do you not think, my friend that the Mushaba Force would play an active role in the upliftment? Do you not think that the Mushaba Force will play a role in pushing Mankind to the next state, the next evolutionary step? Of course there will be an important energy that must be brought into the planet to activate beings to move to the next step (toning of Mushaba). I ask you to connect with the drums, to the beat of the Mother Earth, to go into trance, to go into a circle and let your energy reach to the Ancient Ones. I am Afra and I will stop to see if you have any questions that I might answer for you.

(Q). It was said that you were the overseer of the 1st genetic codes that were introduced into Africa when the Adam species was activated. Please explain.

(A). It means that there was an animal, there was a lower being that was not what you would call man but was more of an" animal" and that there was an evolutionary leap in that animal. The evolutionary leap was the introduction of certain genes into the system. This introduction included a transforming of their genetic codes, of their genes to include new codes. Now in your current technology, your science world would thinks of this as a genetic manipulation if a being from another planet inseminated a women, if you would introduced a cloning structure. But in truth this was done through a spiritual energy. By spiritual energy, I mean that certain life forces can be directed toward the genes and the genes can mutate to the next step in evolution this will allow people to have a higher functioning brain so that they can work on manifesting more.

So to specifically answer your question, there was an over-viewer, an over-seer that, was assisting in this process, to assure that, for example, the proper Beings were chosen, to ensure that they were protected Because it was recognized that when we influenced the development of the species, those who went into higher consciousness may actually be more vulnerable to death and destruction. Because when you begin to think, when you begin to reason and when you begin to have awareness, sometimes you lose part of your animal instincts and there was a need for this protection. So we were involved in assisting in that process.

(Q). It was said that the souls of all people are in danger because of the tragic deaths in Africa. Please explain this statement.

(A). Yes, this means that because of the Aids epidemic, the whole continent and many places, can be annihilated, cultures and connections are being lost. The transmissions of important spiritual practices are being lost. You know that there was the great decimation of the Native Americans and much of their culture was lost. There was the great decimation of many Jewish people in Europe and much of their culture was lost. There were many parts of the world, including the aborigine's world, including the Mayan world, and where this is now happening, On the African continent, you hear the figures of these deaths but you don't really understand that it is also the loss of a culture; it is also the loss of a spiritual connection. These people, many of them, are not able to hold their spiritual connections to the land, their spiritual connections to the world and they do not understand that part of the holding of the Biosphere of life on the planet was based on the energy in Africa. You hear that the rain forest is being destroyed and this is the basis of what is going to be the coming Earth changes. Nobody talks about the destruction of the population in Africa and how that is affecting things.

What I am saying to you is that this is an equivalent, dangerous, destructive pattern that will affect the entire world. Yet the entire world, for example has never appreciated Africa and they have never understood the spiritual connection that Africa has for keeping the planetary life, the planetary biosphere, intact. And now that this is being destroyed, these cultures are being destroyed, there need to be people who are together to hold, to learn what has been done and let the world know. I am not saying this so that you should feel overburdened, but you should understand that it is necessary to preserve as much of this connection, as much of these practices as possible because they are going to be lost. It is like the Native Americans where much of their customs were lost and now they are trying to rediscover them and they do have some connection.

But this connection for the African cultures is not strong in America among the Black peoples. So that I think what is going to have to be accomplished, in part through the transfer, in part through the awareness of the basic fact that the Africans, the African peoples were involved in the first evolutionary leap on this planet for this species. That was one of the most important tasks and now that we are on the precipice, now that we are on the point of another leap, I think that it is important to acknowledge that:

(1). How did the first leap occur?

(2). Who was involved in the first leap?

(3). What is the responsibility when you are going to leap in consciousness and

(4). How do you activate and ensure that the next leap in consciousness, which of course would be a positive leap, will be carried out through the whole planet. Then you begin to understand the Mushaba Force.

You begin to understand that there is a force and energy that needs to go around every person on this planet that is in position to participate in this next leap of consciousness, the next evolution. The evolution in the African continent, it did go quickly, but also many people were killed, many people died who was part of that leap. And this leap of consciousness we need now, just as then, more importantly we need everybody who is open.

What is this next leap of consciousness? It has to do with how many on the planet will make this leap, it has to do with coming into the 5th dimension, and it has to do with the fact that the natives of the planet are going to release certain codes and certain energies to ensure that the planet and the biological offerings on the planet continue.

Why do people not worry about the destruction of Africa? They are so worried about the destruction of other parts of the planet that they do not understand that Africa is the home, the home of the first evolution, the first major evolution into the human Adam people. Archangel Michael wishes to speak to you tonight and unless you have another question for me, I will turn it over to Archangel Michael. Yes I have one more question.

Who are the Mushaba Race?

(A). They're part of a creative race from another planet that came to the Earth to assist in the evolution of the species, the human and they were working with several other higher Beings including the Pleiadians, the Andromedans, and also some of the Sirians. They have connections to external galaxies, namely the Andromedan galaxy. The energy of them is not well known on this planet and they left the planet but have some children or, some shall we say grand children who are connected with them.

(Q). Would that be the Dagon Tribe?

(A). That is possible but I'm not sure that, that tribe has the highest connection. For example, they do not have the knowledge that you have. They do not have the understanding of the 5th dimension that you do. They do not have the understanding of the planetary consciousness. This is Afra and I send you blessings!

<u>The Contribution Of The Black Race To The Human Existence.</u>

The contribution of the Black Race to all Humanity is one of great importance and needs to be understood by all races of humanity. Let us make it clear that the information that is being presented here is not about pointing a finger, or about better or lesser, or any of that ignorance. It is about the truth that needs to be brought foreword. It started a long, long time ago, a very long time ago, way back in the Motherland of Africa and with Black African people. Africa is called the Motherland because it gave birth to all other lands, as the root of civilization. It is the same with Black people who could actually be called the Mother people of the Earth. Because the roots of all humanity, regardless of race, are connected to that of the Black race. So are the genetics, the cellular energy and memories, as well as the molecular structure. It is because of this experiment in genetic re-engineering, that called for the using of the Black race genetics, that we have, today, what is called the human race, the Adam species on this Earth.

Why the Black genetics? Well for many reasons, and one of them being that it provided the best necessary strength and structure of genes needed to re-string the DNA and the genetic codes that would hold a higher frequency of transmutation and evolvement of a species. This evolvement was necessary in order for a lower genetic structured, lower frequency Being to evolve into a higher genetic structured and higher frequency Being, that of the Human Being. The Black genetic structure carried a higher, more powerful charge of genes and DNA that could and would cause the re-structuring of a Being from one level to another higher level. In other words, it was a necessity and, was a profound evolutionary leap that was to become the human race on this planet. Without this happening there would be no human race on the Earth today. Now, the Ascended Being, called Afra, was one of the main overseers of this experiment. He was the watcher and the protector of the evolving species.

Afra Is Troubled

He is very troubled at the serious amount of tragic deaths that are taking place on the continent of Africa. It is an alarming amount of deaths and the true number of these deaths is not honestly being told. What is very important for all people on the Earth to know and understand clearly, is that the destruction of the Black race on the continent of Africa is affecting the very existence of all people on the Earth. According to Afra, no race on this Earth can continue to survive if there are no Black people on the Earth. It is the same as cutting the roots of a tree, all things will lose their potency and life giving substance, and the whole tree dies. The Black race is the root of the tree of civilization and the other races are the stems and braches and leaves. If you kill the root of that tree then you know what happens to the rest of the tree? It is because of the genetics that this happens. Every race has Black genetics and there Black genetics are the root of life of humanity on this planet. This is not to say that other races are any lesser or greater than the Black race because it takes every part to make the whole tree. This experiment involved other races of Beings from other worlds, such as the Pleiades, Andromeda, Sirius.

<u>Sananda</u>

Back To The Land Of Mu

Let us go back to ancient times to the land of Mu. This was a continent where there was a presence on the earth of great Beings. Some were very, very large and were considered giants by today's standards. The land of Mu was based on the co-creation energies. It was based on the ability of a group of people to create a race. Eventually the race became part of the original human race. The human race was begun in two places on this Planet. One was in ancient China and the other was in the ancient forest of the African Area. The ones in ancient China did not thrive They were not able to subsist. The ones in Africa were the primordial coded beings who did have the original genetic codes from the land of Mu and they did have this powerful energy.

It is also true that the Mushaba Force and it is also true that the creation of the original humans onto this planet was done with the assistance of extraterrestrial energies that were working in coalition with the Masters on this planet. The Mushaba Force was able to assist in creation but the Original Beings from Africa were not able to maintain the higher consciousness that was originally implanted into their subconscious through the land of Mu and through the Lemurians.

Therefore, they had to go through a long evolutionary cycle. The African People were basically left to evolve on their own once they were placed in the African Continent. They had to become part of the growing awareness and consciousness on their own and this is, in fact, a part of the great experiment. This is, in fact, a part of the great task that was given and they did accomplish this.

People Of Those Times

My own structures, when I was part of this planet, were tied into the Black African a very dark complexion and many people if they were to see me, as I appeared, would have considered me a Black man. So you know that much of how I looked and much of what image I am to portray to many people was altered. But when you think about the life of even Moses who was also very dark skinned, when you think of all the Israelites, when you think of all of the peoples in those times, they were all coming out of the Black African experience. So you are wishing to connect with an Ascended Master from the African energies and I Sananda am going to work with this channel now so that we can focus, for there were great connections through the ancient Shamans, through the ancient medicine men if you will, throughout the jungles, who were connected into the deep spiritual light. So stay with us while we realign (toning and chanting begins for the realignment).

Chapter 7
A Word From Archangel Michael

Archangel Michael – The Fulfilling of A Mission

Greetings this is Archangel Michael All of the higher beings on this planet are being activated as we are speaking for the raising of the consciousness, for the fulfillment of the mission for which they were brought to this planet. You have been given your instructions, you have been given your activation, and you have been given the tools to work on bringing forth light, bringing forth knowledge, and bringing forth community to many peoples. It is very important for a person to know their mission and it is very important when they can fulfill their mission. So you, my friend, are very blessed at this moment and because of the fact that you are fulfilling your mission, because of the fact that you are following your inner guidance, you are to have wonderful grace, you are going to have wonderful protection, you are going to have wonderful happiness. You are going to have success in your book, you are going to have success in your work and you are going to be fulfilled. So rest assured that this fulfillment, this fulfillment of task, this fulfillment of mission that you have found, is also producing a protective force field around you and the people that you are with who are helping you. You are very healthy and we do not see any health problems. You are very active, you are very energetic and you are very enthusiastic about what you are doing.

Part of this energy is coming from this connection you have with the Mushaba Force, part of this energy is coming from your very strong genes. You have very strong genetic codes for great stamina and this is a reason why you were selected and this is a reason why you are going to follow these instruction that you are receiving, I encourage you to continue to go into trance and I encourage you to continue to connect with higher energy so that you can bring down the information and instructions that you need to bring down. For remember that every one has a unique opportunity to connect with the life force energy that they themselves would understand best. And that means that you have to give yourself the time to meditate, you have to give yourself the time to receive messages especially with writing. As I know you are very excited about your writing, I know that you do automatic writing and I know that you can continue to do automatic writing and work with more light.

Why Not Go Back To The Origin

I would ask you to sit down and write about the connection and the contribution that the African people have made to the world. And as you take the pen in hand with the blank page you are going to have, I will assist you and others will assist you in writing. Because even now, as Afra and Sananda said, it is a very strange occurrence is it not, that people are so excited that, they are into the new age, they are so excited about the Native thinking, but why are they not excited about the Native African thinking? Why do they not go back to the Origin? So, someone has to show them this and I think that you are going to be able to write about this in a way that people will understand and accept. And remember what Sananda said and what Afra said because it is interesting that the Jewish people say that they took on the burden of teaching people about the one God, you have heard this. Well, who took on the burden of the first step in evolution for the human species? Who carried the human code in the stages of development so that the Being that you know now as Human, Mankind developed. People will not understand this, people will laugh but it is true because even then it was a higher spiritual presence that assisted, and I mean this. Blessings to you and your family. This is Archangel Michael, good day.

Chapter 8
A Talk With The Masters

Archangel Michael

A Greater Awareness Is Needed

Let us look at this in a deeper way and let the people of Earth understand the depth of what is being said, why its being said and also the need to have a deeper, greater awareness concerning the terrible tragedy taking place in Africa. It must be understood that, that continent and the people on that continent called Africa are the key to helping all humanity survive on this earth. The untold deaths that occur daily in Africa are a great deal more than what is being told. The deaths re not just by the aids epidemic, this manmade, genetically engineered, virus that was implanted in Africa among the people in order to eradicate them from the face of the earth. Why? Why such madness? It is not only the disease that is killing the people, men, women, children, newborn and unborn, but they are also being wiped out, killed, murdered by the hands of special groups of killers sent to Africa by large corporations and other, handfuls of whites that control. They are out right destroying entire villages of men, women, pregnant women and children and you can bet that this does not make your news media. Not only are the people being killed, murdered, slaughtered and eradicated, but so are the culture, the rituals, the spiritual practices all being wiped from the face of the Earth. All of this is one of the deadliest mistakes that can be made by humanity.

The root of the tree of human civilization is being killed. That which gives life and gave life to the human family species on this planet is being killed off.

So in essence, you allow the roots and the essence to be destroyed. You allow your self to be destroyed. The big problem is that people do not understand this or even believe it. If this does not stop, the entire biosphere of life will be thrown out of balance and the people of Earth will perish. This is how serious this is. The people of the Earth cannot survive without the African people and without the land of Africa, because that is the connection, the foundation of human life on this planet.

Another thing that is not in balance and is unnatural is that the Black people in America do not hold a strong connection to the people, the roots or the land of Africa. The Blacks in America need to become aware of the necessity to, not just get in touch with their roots, but to connect deeply with their roots, their heritage and their homeland. There is a deep need for them to know and understand the ancient spiritual native practices, and rituals, and to feel the soil and know the spirit of the Earth on that continent. American Black people, for the most part, and in particular the youth, are not interested in knowing their roots.

There is no strong influence on them to know or connect with their history. Black people in America are so involved in accepting this American life and connecting with false cultures that they have no true desire to know their Homeland or their Native people or their Ancestors. There are reasons why this is so. It is due to brainwashing of their culture, programming not to love themselves and the psychological affects from slavery. Let me explain to you some of the things that contribute to this great travesty of the people by the people.

Why Not A Strong Connection

There are many reasons why the Black people in America do not have a strong connection. Yes some of it is due to the affects of slavery which cover a great deal of ground. Part of that damage has to do with not wanting to be connected with an event that is very demeaning, an event that put a people in a class lower than that of the animal kingdom, an event that destroys self-esteem and pride. So people of the Black race and, again, particularly the young, are not interested in hearing about their ancestors being slaves and that their roots and heritage is founded in slavery. We know that this is very far from the truth. The heritage of the Black race is founded on many great kings and Queens and rulers on this Earth. The Black people heritage and roots are found in being the root of the tree of humankind's existence. The roots of Black spirituality, of Black galactic spirituality, comes from a race of majestic beings called the Mushaba race from planet Mushaba. Slavery was just an aspect of what they went through but that is not their history. It is something to be very proud of and to have great self-esteem about. Think of how a people are able to go through such tragic events for over 400 years and still survive and still maintain a certain connection with deep spirituality.

There were wonderful inventions that were invented by certain Black people and they were not given credit but someone else took the credit. The founding of certain things through the study of science and medicine that they were not given credit for and someone else took the credit. There is much non- recorded history that humanity is not aware of which is why we are bringing forth this information of the great contribution of the Black race to the existence of humanity. There is the psychological damage that has been talked about in an earlier chapter. We know how powerful those affects are on the minds of people. Then there is this wanting to have pride and saying that "I am not a slave, my ancestors were but not me, I am an American and that doesn't have anything to do with me." This is a cry out for understanding. The Black people do not really search and study their roots and it is not a tradition among Black families to do this and it should be. They should be connected to this when they are the youngest of children. But what also has to happen is that they need to be told the whole story about their heritage and not just the slave story. The slave story is simply one chapter in the book.

You also have so many Blacks wanting to fit into society that they shun or disown their roots. Some are ashamed, which is very unfortunate, because there is nothing at all to be ashamed about. Many Black people are so busy trying to survive from one day to the next they don't see any importance or necessity or urgency to study about their roots. They wonder how this will help me eat and pay my bills and raise my family etc. There are many Blacks who try not to have anything to do with Black people but want to surround themselves with White friends and associates. There are those who experience success and begin to live and act in the manner of their white counterparts and try to drop the blackness. This is really not a good thing.

This is why we ask Anakhanda and those who are working with him to take on this project, as a part of their mission, and bring awareness to humanity about the contribution to humanity by the Black race.

Papa Shabazz

Greetings and Mushaba Blessings to you my ancestor of modern times; I am Papa Shabazz the one who is within your lineage and heritage of life. It is true that my blood flows through you at this time. You have come from a great line of teachers and leaders, some of which are not all known in your world. I am the one who saw into what you call the future time ahead. I was given a vision by an Archangel, who showed me what was to lie ahead for the Black people of Africa. I saw a terrible vision of horror, untold deaths and destruction of my people. It was unbelievable and so I called together the elders of the people and took counsel with them. Many of them did not accept or believe what I told them and thought that I was losing my mind. I said to them that I would bring it to the people and let them decide for themselves about what I proposed. I called the people together and told them of my vision about the future of our people and what we were to face. I told them that we had to prepare now for the hardships that were coming to our people and it would take time, it would take generations of preparation. Many of the people who I spoke to, to explain the vision that I was give by the Archangel, also thought that I was out of my mind, But there were some who thought that I was very sane and believed that I had these warnings and had a mission to accomplish. Those who understood and wanted to take part in this great mission all gathered together with me and we left the community of people and went to live in the very, very tough conditions of the jungles. Thus we became the tribe of Shabazz

The Move To The Jungles

We had to undergo many years and generations of growth, development and adaptation to the very difficult hardships of jungle life. We had to work day in and day out to cultivate the jungle land to grow food. We had to find means of survival from the very harsh and deadly elements and had to learn to be able to survive with the threat of being attacked and eaten by the various predators in the jungle. We had to adjust to eating things that we were not used to and living in close tight conditions for our safety. We had it very difficult and this adaptation passed through our genes and DNA to our children and to their children and so forth. Various factions begin to form, and little by little villages began to form. Some had different ways and customs than others. But it got to the point in evolution lets say, to where we were able to deal with great harshness and great difficulty. We were able to deal with the death of loved ones at the hands of wild animals. We learned so many valuable lessons that were needed for our future survival. Many even died from the hardships of that life but each generation became stronger and more powerful. We knew what it was like to be separated from people we loved. We knew what it was like to have to adapt to a new way of living and a new environment. All this lead up to the time when the White race was coming to fulfill what I had seen.

There is more to this story than what I have given and there will be more details, that are not mentioned at this time, that will come forth. I will be with you hence forth, We will communicate more often and I will bring you history that is not known. My peace and love to you.

The Name Shabazz

The name Shabazz goes back to Machu Picchu of Peru and it also involved the entire continent of Mu, the total circumference of the world before it was split into continents. It means that you are teachers and masters, and that you signify with that name. The letter S that incurs in the ways of spirit and that you'll find that the letters also send out a specific vibratory rating in respect to the different lifetimes that you have had and where your place in the world is now and where that name is implied are the helpers and teachers as you world enters it's great changes that lie ahead of you. The name Shabazz has it's origin in other worlds. It comes from the Dharma and Medinian concepts of infinitude where the name Shabazz has it's origin. Here you'll find it within the Dharmic process which is that of the light forces where in the creation of your identity was in one of the 98 planets surrounding the central infinitude.

So you'll find that as you say it, even verbalize it to yourself and others, it has a specific attraction that draws to you individuals that are seeking the teaching abilities though within them, and the abilities still will have there merit as you move toward the fulfillment of your life. There were one who was a Master by the name of Shabazz that had something to do with separating the Earth and the moon and some of those same Masters are present now in your Earth life. Shabazz is a name that also registers back into the ancient Silks and the Shardians ancient civilizations but he can't be named as one responsible solely for the change or the splitting of planets because he was one of the group of so called scientist that had consented toward these changing ways of using pranic force but not understanding its repercussions. Thus the responsibility cannot be assumed by one but he would have contributed his part in the changes in the circumference of energies but not to what there is karma involved upon those who carry the same energy name.

There is a group of these masters by that name and they move more within the specific processes of your life at anytime of the past that you have been involved with them. It invites you to a more fuller focus of your intent and purposes and you will find a ring of this mystical force that draws to you not only those things which are in the pathway of your fulfillment but also give measure to your self realization of service you'll give to all those around you. Also Shabazz is seen in the energies as I told you before as Bazai. Bazai means the full illuminations to the garden of energies to which will attract you to a specific rating of which you do not see or understand at the present time. And I leave that at the present because of your own spiritual travels which will answer many of those concerns in regard to names because there is a connection with Mushaba, Shabazz, Absheema, and Bazai. In the original meaning of the name also you will find that it is said in opposite syllables and your original meaning of Shabazz is Barshay. This is from the force of the samurai of your beginning your work in foreign shores and which the name implies a fullness and expansion of the oneness of life.

Ascended Master Sophia

Greetings to you, I am Sophia an Ascended Master of the feminine persuasion. I have been in contact with you before in other lifetimes. I come now because of the very important work that you are doing. I will be participating in this work and we will have the opportunity to speak many times together about the tragedy of what is happening in the continent of Africa. I will share information with you concerning the role of the female in the African life and the feminine perspective of God/Goddess. We are very closely united in energy together and you vibrate, that is the feminine part of your being in which everyone has both aspects, you vibrate in balance with my energy and I only represent another part or aspect of yourself. We will speak of how the men in the world today, regardless of race, are missing the very important recognition of the feminine aspect that they all have, that needs to be cultivated. It is too much overlooked because the true understanding is not there. We will speak about the role of the feminine principle in the future of your Earth. We are not speaking about in particular, the female role, we are speaking about the feminine aspect, same as not the male but the masculine aspect. Men and women have both aspects within them but for the most part they go totally unrecognized.

There are many reasons for this and we will talk about some of them as we communicate more often. I have been known as a Goddess energy and I possess great wisdom, knowledge and power. I have much to bring forward that was not known before. I have much to bring forward about the female and the feminine that is not known by anyone, including those of the feminine body. It is not a separation between feminine and masculine as it is made out to be. One only chooses to accept the robe of flesh over the spirit to express in body form a particular aspect of the Self. This is decided according to what you have to do in the world, and other circumstances that we will discuss, as well. It doesn't matter the body worn to the Earth world to do your work and there is far too many distinctions being propagated between the two bodies.

All must learn to come into the fullness of themselves, by accepting their bi-sexual nature, that of having both aspects within you. When you can merge them together as one and not overlook one for the other, then you become what many are seeking all there lives that which is completion. You will never find it by two people coming together. It must be found within the self first, before two come together, both as complete beings, one to the other. We will explain more about this at another talk together. Peace and love to you my dear.

Arthur Comments

I said to you that the feminine principle would play a very important role in the future of your Earth. The feminine role is one of nurturing. Nurturing has so many aspects to it and some of them are not recognized. Nurturing does not only mean the raising of children, cooking and cleaning and all the material duties of the female mother. We are speaking here of the feminine principle, which has no gender. Feminine is not gender, feminine energy is energy that could materialize into a physical female body which is only a more natural receptacle to house that energy physically if you particularly want to express that quality or aspect of being in a material way. The same applies to the masculine energy. The feminine energy is something that is natural to the physical bodies of both female and male. Only the female, as said, expresses more of that principle and the male more of the masculine principle, but they both exist together in the same body as a oneness.

The feminine energy is a deeper spiritual sense of knowing an energy that represents a nurturing of the spiritual side of existence, and a nurturing of your natural abilities of expressing Divine love, of bringing forward the sensitive side of your spiritual nature. The sensitive side of your spiritual nature is the aspect that is very loving, very nurturing, very intuitive, very deeply in touch with the spiritual side of life. It is the side of your self that is much more deeply in touch with your inner being and open to the spiritual nuances of life. Now this ability is inherent in both men and women, but it is a little more inclined toward the female, because she embodies this feminine aspect in material body same as the male is more inclined to express the masculine qualities which by the way, are very wonderful qualities that are inherent in the female as well. It's not to say that the male cannot be as sensitive, or in touch spiritually as a female, or be as intuitive and so forth.

The reason that, for the most part, it is not so is because the male shuns or locks out that part of himself for the so called sake of being masculine. He has a misconception about that as well. The male has to open up to the feminine principles within him in order to continue to survive. You will see so many males dying from brain aneurisms, and heart attacks because they are resisting their feminine nature, which wants and needs to express itself. The heart is opening whether they want it or not. The male for the most part feels scared and uneasy about expressing sensitivity, about saying one to another, I love you and actually feel that love. They are uneasy about hugging another male in a loving way but are very good actors in their manly ways of hugging which is really a very poor attempt, at best, at hugging. Who told them that it was not the way of the male to express sensitivity? They got it all wrong. They think that expressing the feminine nature means not being a man, or That it would make them soft, or what they term gay. All this is nonsense and far from the truth. It is a necessity for the feminine energy to be more in balance because it has been so suppressed for so long. It is the energy of great wisdom that needs to come in and move into a position to where both the feminine and masculine can operate in a oneness and harmony of life. Then they can live their lives with true direction and purpose.

This feminine energy has been missing in your world but now is coming forth in great waves, and everyone must open up to it, even the females. Yes, there are many females who do not express the feminine energy because they have gotten away from it due to all this women is equal to men movement and other things. They are not 100% into their role either and some of them even express more of the masculine energy than feminine energy.

There are imbalances everywhere on the Earth that must come into balance and harmony. The leap into the higher dimensions requires it and you cannot make that leap without it. You will either be left behind or move into the energies of life or what you call death. The feminine energy is a higher, finer vibration that is more suited for the higher frequencies. This does not mean that the male cannot reach that vibration. It is as I have said, that the male only needs to move into the acceptance of his feminine energy within and allow it to cohabitate, to blend, to meld with the masculine.

The time of all this head strength and brawn, and male oriented and dominated thinking and action, is coming to an end because it is out of balance. There was a time when there was too much of a dominant feminine energy in the world, which did not work either. This is why there has to be a balance with the two, which is really one. In the higher realms of understanding, there is no male or female, but more of what you would call androgyny, and even beyond that, there is nothing but energy, light and frequency. I have to leave now but I will return to continue our conversation. Love and Blessings to you, this is Ascended Master Sophia.

Chapter 9
Questions And Answers

This chapter is filled with questions and answers that will give a great deal of information that we fell would serve the readers. We felt that since so much information came with the answers we should share this with everyone.

(Q). What was my name during the time of King Tut and Pharaoh Amenhotep?

(A). Here we find in your expression of life is one that served in rulership along with the Pharaohs. One that was entwined within the artistic nature of rulership and here your name was Abinook and that calls to you from these past experiences. Speaking of it or reflecting upon it, draws it closer into your nature and to your force, and above all, to the fuller understanding of your Spiritual Self.

(Q). There were these different plans drawn up concerning Black people and some of the former presidents were involved and aware of these plans. Now that they are in spirit, how is it that they come and speak through different channels as if they are all good and spiritual, how is this allowed?

(A). Because they are what you call the wolves in sheep's clothing. Don't forget, your world vibrates in that word deceit that is popular in all avenues of your commercialized ways of living and each one is constantly being a parasite on another. But then looking at it again more deeply it makes no difference. It will have its complete defeat, i.e. because it does not wear the full meaning of Truth which is another word for God. I'd not be concerned about it. But you will find, to emphasize this condition is that your civil war was not fought over slavery. It was a strictly political concern, and therefore, it does not merit the truth of liberating the Black people. And don't forget, other races have found themselves in the same quandary. Your business however, is more within the spiritual warrior services that lie ahead of you, if you choose to do so.

(Q). What can be done to totally eradicate Aids from the continent of Africa?

(A). Yes, it is possible to heal any sickness. The belief and the manifestation of sickness, is a belief and manifestation in a lack of love. When the body, mind and spirit believes that it is suffering from a lack of love, it is out of balance and harmony with itself and it is in disease. What happens, is that the human, consciously or otherwise, betrays itself to one degree or another and the body reflects that betrayal. The body hasn't betrayed the Self it is just that the human is believing with all its power and might in sickness and disease and being unlovable. So what heals the disease is the willingness to believe in the power of love. This, again, is how Jesus and other Masters healed the individuals in their time that were suffering from illusion. Aids are particularly challenging of course, but what it, is, is that you are asking for help collectively. The whole human race is asking for help to evolve. And so, that hunger and thirst for spiritual understanding of themselves, and the belief that there is such spiritual understanding, manifests in ways like this. Also, of course, it is transmitted through sexual activity, and that acting out sexually when there isn't truly the presence of love, also magnetizes individuals for this kind of a vibration. The best thing that you could do is to send them pink light from your heart center. See all who consider themselves to be ill and offer them, through their higher selves a message, that in truth, they are perfect whole, and complete. You offer your love, and the love of the universe through you, on the vibration of this pink light, to help them to heal themselves and to love themselves. Work with this in a group, and as individuals, on a consistent basis and it will begin to magnetize and manifest change in that situation.

There are individuals, right now, walking your world that have gone from negative to positive, or vice versa, and from illness to health with this condition who have healed themselves. It is just that its not talked about, like many things in your world are not talked about, but they have healed themselves through loving themselves and letting themselves be loved. There isn't an illness that exists on this planet in which the individual isn't suffering from a lack of love. There isn't one situation where the willingness to love and be loved wouldn't improved the situation. Just by holding that vibration, there is no such thing as an incurable disease.

(Q). The Ancient Elders from Africa, where are they now?

(A). They are definitely available to all those who want to help humanity with the help of the African Elders. The name that they give us to use is the Council of the Ancient Ones, in order to have a vibration to work with. The Council of the Ancient Ones says that they are very proud of you and your commitment to bring this message out to the world in this lifetime, in the ways that you have done, and will do, and they thank you for asking for them. They say to work with the golden light in your visualizations, to begin with, and also to connect with them, as well. Call upon the Council of the Ancient Ones and attune to their vibration, which all, who wish to, can do. You have been working with them already and we understand your wanting to share this blessing with all humanity. This Council of Ancient Ones is a part of the Mushaba Energy and you have worked with them in many other ways, as well. You, like others on the pathway of spiritual light, have been asking for this deepening connection and it is available to those who seek it. Humanity has to allow itself to trust what it is feeling, because a lot of people are opening up to a lot of emotional power and the ability to manifest. Manifesting is the thoughts and feelings aligned perfectly in harmony with the soul's desire. The energy of the Ancient Ones is certainly supportive and is assisting in this manifesting, that is taking some into the process of moving into the miracles and the success, and all of that. They surround you, and we see the number 12.

We see 12 Beings and bring in the Golden Light and sit with the Council of 12 of the Ancient Ones, along with Archangel Michael, in your meditations. A part of surrender that humanity must understand is simply going to sleep at night and as they wake up surrender into a deeper experience. In this way your consciousness is being attuned so you can have easier access to other messages. You are already a very gifted and a qualified channel in your own right and this is for sure.

(Q). Explain the difference between Afra, the life stream and Afra, the group consciousness for our readers.

(A). A life stream is your soul's journey, the energy of your soul moving from lifetime to lifetime. Things are much more permeable on the other side of the dimensions here. The group consciousness is the energy of a group that supports your life stream. Your soul journey, but not necessarily a part of that particular soul vibration. They interact, they inter-relate, and the group consciousness of Afra is what we get, the Council of the Ancient Ones. In this lifetime, everyone has a role to play if they decide to play it and a part of your many roles, is to bring this spiritual message back to humanity, particularly to those people in the world that have forgotten that they are a Spiritual Beings having a physical experience. You carry in your soul's vibration, in your life stream, the dignity, the worthiness, and the courage that are a part of the Ancient Ones.

(Q). Where is the Spirit of Shaka Zulu?

(A). He is still in the dimensions and he is a part of your field of energy as well. You say the name and he is there, a powerful energy, the warrior energy, leadership energy, kingly energy. He is there absolutely. You see, this is the energy that humanity is healing, that of illusion and separation. Honestly, there is nothing that you can imagine, there's nothing you can dream about, nothing that you can envision that wouldn't be available to you in some form of reality. So you are interested in the Ancient Ones, you are interested in Shaka Zulu, you are interested in Ascended Master Mushaba and these Beings are there the minute you focus upon them. This is what humanity needs to know and understand. They are not in time and space, they are in spirit. So, they are always available to you.

It is our greatest joy to see Human Beings who are evolving there consciousness back to the place from

Ascended Masters of Color - Ascended Beings of Light

which they have come which is that energy of oneness that you have channeled so beautifully in your book. So whenever anyone focuses on their energies, they will be available to them. You are a clear channel and there are deeper and different other levels of expression that you are working towards. So just knowing this and understanding the context of those things that they are not cut and dry, they are separate, but they are all available to you and to humanity. And, as you are in service to humanity, certainly they are very much in service to you.

(Q). What can you tell about Papa Shabazz and my lineage with him.

(A). Well, the feeling here is that you made a commitment in that lifetime with Papa Shabazz, to end suffering on this plane of consciousness and this lifetime is about the completion of that commitment. In other words, more Beings will come to the realization in this lifetime that they are Spiritual Beings, and they are creating their own reality that they can end their own suffering, any that they have ever experienced in this world. So, you made a commitment in that lifetime as a healer and as a very compassionate Being to do whatever is necessary, whatever it takes, to heal the suffering of the world, because it moved you that deeply.

What your guides want you to remember is that you also are a part of the world whose suffering is being transcended. In the process of healing the suffering of the world, also surrender and release your suffering, your attachments to the illusion. Humanity wonders all the time, when will they achieve enough love and enough healing to come back to God.

The moment they allow themselves to realize that they are Divine energy, not simply in this form of body, and in this time and space, and as they so do, moment by moment, they move back to themselves, back to God. Not only are you here to heal humanity's suffering, you are here to heal your own illusions, as well. And yours are equally as deserving as theirs. And truly, when you do heal your own, you heal the world and that is the gift of the human journey.

(Q). What is the message of the Lion Head on the Sphinx. From a race of Beings who look like the image of the Sphinx?

(A). Well yes, they is a race of Beings and all animals of your world are in the image and likeness of some form of life brought forward out of Creator as a humanity. There are bird beings, snake beings, lions, dolphins and all the rest. Part of the journey here is growing and evolving. This world was created as a place of forgetting, so that you could grow, through the process of remembering. The lion head on the Sphinx represents, astrologically, Leo, the sign of Leo and the virgin, Leo and Virgo, the women and the lion, the masculine and the feminine, the humble and the exalted and all of that balancing together in symbolic form to remind humanity of it's true nature. So there are energies in the Sphinx, Etherically.

There are entities, who are conscious Beings, connected to that field of consciousness, both in time and space, and outside time and space, that will make their presence known. You have a relationship with these beings, as you know, and this is why you asked the question. You are wanting to have a greater understanding of the largest, possible picture of things. The Sphinx is called the Place of the Lion. You, can and will work with these beings, the Lion Beings. You can call them just by going into your meditation, and I believe you have done this. Focus on the energy of the Sphinx, like the pyramids that sit across the field from the Sphinx. These are activating energies like the crop circles that are appearing on your planet. These are sacred because they remind you of your true nature A Mandela is the same thing, that which inspires you, that which uplifts you, that which deepens your consciousness.

So, we simply suggest that you transport yourself, in your minds eye, to the Sphinx and sit in that vibration and call upon those energies, those beings and play with the energy and see how it would present more of itself to you. Again, it is so beautiful that you have come to a place in your growth that will decide that beforehand. You can declare that you are safe and you are respected in every environment. Now we can work with you as an equal, and with these other beings as well. They are primal, archetypal and unique unto themselves. These are the energies that you are looking to connect with, that are also a part of what is available to you at this time.

(Q). What are your suggestions about the title of the book that I am writing on the Black race?

(A). It feels fine. We suggest the term African because part of what is happening right now on the planet is this process of Aids in Africa and this is like September 11th. This is the heart of humanity crying out and asking for support. What you are doing through your work, those of you of the Mushaba Force, is bringing people back in touch with the Ascended Master consciousness that is connected to your race, the African race in this lifetime. You were other races in other lifetimes, obviously, but there was a particular focus that you wanted to focus on in this lifetime which connects to that past life that we discussed earlier about Papa Shabazz, that begin in that vibration, and wants to bring things to a completion in a similar vibration. So we suggest that somewhere in the terms of the title, you use African because there is such a beautiful healing that is preparing to happen in the races, in the differences between people.

You are definitely in service to that in this lifetime. Anything that can allow the differences to be seen in the light of their true nature, and well, black is a bit of a slang term. The whole emphasis here, as far as we are concerned, is to return dignity, to return the intrinsic worthiness, because this is what the African sacrificed itself for. Just as the Indian race did in your country, sacrificed itself for the return to this balance, and by that we mean they played a role and you played a role and roles were played that created the imbalances, so they can be seen, so they can be healed.

You are now in the lifetime of healing the imbalances on this planet. There is a heart opening that is happening on the part of humanity and as long as there are ways that people can be invited into this process, it will move forward very beautifully. This is why we say that the slang term is a bit disconnecting for some people that you want to be connecting with who were African in another lifetime and who will very much support what you are doing. They are compassionate, they are evolved, and they are enlightened beings and all of humanity needs to be taken care of. You will have a large audience for your message and present it in the way that connects people.

Chapter 10
I Am Your Brother - I Am Your Sister

This is about the unity that is inherent within all humanity, that of oneness, that of brotherhood and sisterhood. This was the message of the Master Afra, 500,000 years ago. He simply stated, "I Am Your Brother." He wanted all to know that the need to be and to live as brothers and sisters was paramount. It would be easy if people of the Earth would believe in the simple truths such as: want for your brother and sister that which you want for yourself, or do unto your brother and sister as you would have done to you. These are simple powerful truths and if humanity followed them in the spirit of it and lived it, this planet would accelerate overnight and the violence and the hatred and the separation would cease to exist overnight.

There are too many separations that divide and mainly it is because we do not treat each other or see each others as brothers and sisters. We only recognize the biological blood connection as brothers and sisters and anything outside of that doesn't have much chance, if any. Not to see all humanity as brothers and sisters is the trick that we all have gotten caught up in. It is the lie that we have been told, and, has been accepted by humanity, for generations of time. Many people actually thrive off this separation and this attachment to their own blood family. Humanity has been given so many examples that show that brotherhood and sisterhood is the true way.

The Gift Brought To Humanity

Not only was Master Afra an example but many other Great Ones as well. If you take a good close look at the Black race and what gifts they bring to all humanity is that of brotherhood and sisterhood. Now it is true that Black people do not as a whole practice and live that as they once did long ago. They have been tricked and robbed of that truth and it is evident as you look at the Black people and how they respond to each other, as a whole. Let me explain what I mean here. There was a time when Black people openly accepted all people into their lives and saw them as brothers and sisters. The Blacks, even today, still call people, whether they are white, black, red, yellow, brown etc. brother and sister. The Black people are the motivating factor behind other races referring to each other as brother and sister. This principle, this natural way is inherent among the Black people and is a part of the teachings that the Black race were to bring to humanity. It is unfortunate that the Black people have gotten into this trick of separation and the blatant violence and killing of one another is true evidence to this truth.

Imagine if you would, what it would be like if all humanity, regardless of race and differences would call each other, see, each other and treat each other, as brother and sister. It is something that must transpire and it must be an unstoppable movement among humanity to make this a reality.

Brotherhood And Sisterhood Is Oneness

Brotherhood and sisterhood is oneness, love, unity in all diversity. The human family is just like the small family unit. With in it are many differences among the brothers and sisters but yet, they do not separate because of these differences. They still see each other and treat each other as family. It is no different with the human family. The differences are diverse and we use them to judge and hate, to dislike and separate, and to make excuses for why we treat people the way we do. This is what the new age is about, brothers and sisters of Earth, the recognition and acceptance of each other as such. This separation will not be allowed into the higher dimensions and people who are not in this acceptance have to understand that you cannot call themselves Masters or achieve their Masterhood, without being in balance with this truth.

The question is, do those on the spiritual pathway, who interact with other races of people and call each other brother and sister, do they really fully, unconditionally, deep within feel this to be true? Without any kind of feelings that may not be the same, that lets say the White race would feel toward each other when they call each other brother and sister, or those of the Black race or any other race who call each other that. A lot of times it is lip service and a lot of times it is a moment of being caught up in a righteous feeling. Sometime those words are spoken but when a choice is to be made between the race that you represent and the race that another represents, what choice will be made and will it be because of color.

Will you make the choice to choose only that which is colorless and right, as the heart sees it? Because, the heart is colorless. Instead of saying, I am on the side of this or that race, why not say, that, I, am on the side of the human family, the human race. Basically, what I am saying here is that we need to come to the understanding that, I am your brother and I am your sister, and live that understanding everyday of our lives. And until humanity accepts this, and sees this truth, there will not be the balancing and harmony necessary to move onward into higher consciousness.

There is no Master who is truly a Master Ascended or otherwise, who does not see all as brothers and sisters of one race and one family. Realize that these feelings that we have toward each other as races are taught feelings and beliefs and are not natural in any way.

<u>Children Are Not Born Prejudice</u>

When children are first born into this world, no matter the race they choose to be born in, for whatever reasons of mission, or cause and effect. They have no feelings of separation or hatred for another person whose color is different. They are taught these things as they grow in life. If you were to take a child from all races, and the parents of each of theses races were prejudice against each other because of race differences, and you allowed them to grow up together, without the influence of negative taught behaviors, they would grow up without prejudice toward each other due to racial differences. They would not even notice the differences other than the fact that they are different flavors or colors from each other, otherwise they would feel that they are pretty much the same. You can take another child, raise them and teach them the prejudicial views and attitudes and they will grow up to be prejudicial.

Understand that no one is born prejudiced, or born in hatred toward another. It is the children that are born today that will break down, and destroy this barrier of lies for all humanity.

The Indigo Children Cannot Be Corrupted

The indigo children that are being born and born in mass in every race on the planet Earth will come without the separation and the hatred and the prejudices toward their brother or sister. Regardless of how much the family of these children try to teach them this negative way, it will, only serve to strengthen them toward the oneness of life. It will not take effect, because they are being born with a more open and activated set of codes, which do not limit in the same way as the codes of their parents and their parents before them did. These children are seeing each other as brothers and sisters and really truly have no ill feelings toward another because of color. They are the ones who will stand up for the human family. They will say to their parents, their family, and their friends, regardless of race differences," I Am Your Brother and I Am Your Sister!" Notice how the youth population is really into each other more and more, the dress, the music, and the social gatherings.

The evidence is there and nothing that anyone can do will change that fact because this is a part of the Divine timing, of the Divine plan. The Divine plan will be fulfilled. As long as there is separation there can be no peace and unconditional love on Earth. The youth of today are considered by many, to be rebellious but I see them as the pioneers, the warriors who are not going to accept this old negative way of separation and lack of brotherhood and sisterhood any more. They are tired of it and have come here to tear this down. That is what they are rebelling against. The old, outdated, wrong, negative, established ways of life that only serve to promote more separation. They are masters at doing their job. If you want to move forward, and really be about the work of the Creator, then it is time to wake up to the Truth of, "I Am Your Brother, I Am Your Sister!"

Chapter 11
Africa Needs Change

Change of Traditions

There are certain traditions in Africa that need to be changed. If the continent of Africa and it's people are to survive, there needs to be a change in the way the women of Africa are treated and viewed. The old past traditions are out dated and have no place in the ever expanding consciousness of humanity. The women are not, and should not be treated, as inferior beings. They are too important to the health, growth and expansion of the people in Africa and the blending and balancing of the feminine and masculine principles of Creation. The God/Goddess energy is awakening very strongly on this planet and women of all races, religions and traditions are stepping out and fighting to get out from under the old ways of how they are viewed and treated by the men of their particular association. The treating of the women, as if they are mere property, and can be brought and sold for as little as a cow or a few chickens, is very crude and outdated and very unappreciated. This is no way to respect the energy of a Goddess, the Mother of Civilization. There needs to be a greater awakening among the male population in Africa and understanding that the women can no longer be treated and discarded like an old dish of rotten flesh. They are, as stated, very vital to the Race of the African people. They carry the Goddess energy which is necessary, because of the time we are now in and are moving more deeply. The energy of the heart is here and it is bringing about the balance between feminine and masculine, God and Goddess.

The Understanding Of Men Must Change

The concept that many African men have is very faulty and they need to be taught the true understanding and awareness of what they have in their women. The understanding that men are better, and that women are here to serve man and their needs and pleasures, is truly wrong and out of balance with the Universal Laws of Life and Creation. This traditional understanding and concept needs to be changed and the Universal Law taught to the youth, as children, so they can affect the vital changes in attitude toward the women of Africa. This, of course, needs to be of paramount importance, for all women the world over.

I see how they are looked at in the eyes of the men, and particularly, the young males of Africa. They are seen with untrue, lying eyes, as pleasure slaves and servants. This entire imbalance that is being created on the continent of Africa and among the people is dangerous. It is dangerous to the full sovereignty and freedom of Africa, and it will destroy the continent and it's people, if these imbalances are not put into balance with the Law. It is already adding to the division of the people and society, because they frown upon women who want equality and freedom to choose their own direction in life. They no longer want to be bartered off, or arranged to be given to someone who they do not know or care for or even have a say so about. They are taken away at the age of puberty and some as young as ten years old. They are basically slaves to the man and do all the major, heavy work while the man sits and does nothing. In some traditions the women have to get up and give their seat to the man when he walks into the room. All this is out of balance and it will tear the fabric of African society apart, if it does not change. A man can take a young girl away from her home at 13 or 14 years old and if he gets tired of her, can send her back home with all the children and think nothing of it. The man does not see or care about his responsibility to her and the children or how this can, and may very well, ruin the women's life. The rights of women in Africa, and in the world for that matter, should be strongly supported.

However, there needs to be a clear understanding of the direction women are going in, and they must have the proper understanding and awareness of their responsibility, as well. It must not get out of balance on their part. There has to be a mutual agreement between men and women of African. They can maintain their cultures and traditions, with the necessary adjustments that remove the outdated and unfair treatment of the women in African society. Also with the rampant ravaging of Aids in Africa, the men need to be a lot more aware of their sexual actions and not go from women to women with no thought of the consequences that are involved. It is a major killer in Africa. Already there are over ten million orphans in Africa due to Aids. There are children born with it. According to recent reports, at the time of this writing, every 60 seconds, 11 cases of Aids are contracted in the world and of those 11, 10 of them are contracted in Africa. This is just unbelievable, and it must without failure, be rectified. This should be a true call to all humanity, to come to the aid of the Motherland of the planet. Remember, if Africa dies, the planet of humanity dies as well.

Chapter 12
PASSING THE MANTLE OF KNOWLEDGE

The Youth Of Africa-What Is Happening

The youth of Africa is moving away from the traditions of knowledge, to grasp the traditions of the American - European culture. This is nothing short of a tragedy for the African culture. There is a great deal of knowledge that at one time was always passed down from grandfather to father and from father to son. The knowledge that was being passed down was of such incredible substance and power that kept it, the power and stability of the tribe's culture and knowledge and the ability to continue, intact. The youth, at one time, looked forward to the passing of this knowledge. Nothing was more important or had more meaning and purpose in life than this because it was necessary in continuing the heritage, integrity, and lifeline of the tribe and of the family essence now, it is all but lost. What has happened to the youth that caused them to look away from their roots of power and wisdom to outside, limiting pursuits of material attainments?

How were they lost in the illusions of what was being offered to their outer, sensual, ego mind, instead of their inner higher mind? What is it that has so much pull and so much power to make them shun, and even feel embarrassed about, their heritage and their primal way of life? How could they not hold on to such great power of this knowledge, that is more valuable then any amount of material possessions? There is a great powerful influence that has entered the structure and foundation of African culture that has corrupted the base of their beliefs and way of life that has its uniqueness in the spiritual energy of existence.

Money or any amount of material accomplishments cannot stand on the same ground, as the power and wisdom of the Primal Forces of the African Ceremonies and Rituals. That which was being passed down was of the greatest value a people could have and it is something that cannot be taken away from you as a material possession. It is within you and there it remains, at your command, to come forward with great wisdom and power.

The sad thing is that the African elders are dying off and taking with them this great wealth of knowledge and wisdom and power, as well as the immeasurable power and purpose of ritual and ceremony, Which has no equal on the Earth. Many African youth don't want to hear it, nor have the time and interest, in what their ancestors had and passed forward. They are too busy chasing the falsities of life. They are wanting to live in the most imbalanced and emotionally disrupted places on the Earth, which are the cities. They want to get the electronics and entertainment and clothing and all the glamour that they have been sold on. The youth have been caught up, drawn in, and mentally infiltrated by the media, and by the European ways of life, and all the glitter, this is how they measure success in life. They measure the importance of life by: How many possessions do you have? How much money do you make? What kind of clothes do you wear? What do you believe in? Do you believe in that old African ritual and nonsense and do you still follow those old outdated ways of your ancestors?

These are the things that the youth are facing everyday. They are being told that their ways are outdated, no good and embarrassing, to these young hip youth. All this superstition of our ancestors and their old ways don't fit with the modern day way of life. All these detrimental lies and tricks are being fed and accepted. The idea here is to put a stop to the power, of the people and in particular the people of Africa. Look at the great length that modern day man has gone to, to disrupt the natural way of African life. Look at the power of influence that has been cast in the minds of these youth, who are taught that there parents and grandparents are old and stuck in ways that are no longer sensible in today's society.

The youth are made, and taught in their education and through the media, to feel embarrassed and ashamed of what and who they are. So, the youth do not want to learn the old ways, which are not old ways, but the natural way of life. They do not feel that their culture and heritage is offering them anything of value because it is not a material possession. Many, many elders are dying with a great burden of knowledge that should have been left behind to their people.

What happens is that after enough of this the culture and heritage starts to die, and then before you know it, it becomes a story of myth and fairytales. There is no more power, only empty practice that is a shell of what it was. And that which the youth have had all their lives, as a normal way of life, is now being shunned for the abnormal, unnatural ways of life. They are taking it all for granted because of what they have been lead to believe. It is so easy to lead these youth in the wrong direction because of the great power of media and false education.

Educated Out Of Their Minds

They are being educated right out of their minds, right out their culture and heritage, right out of their sense of the oneness and the power within themselves. This in itself is powerful enough to destroy them, without them seeing that they are being destroyed. It takes them out of their natural selves, and so they live a falsehood of life, that never gives them that inner feeling of satisfaction that they are searching for in the material ways of life. Their spirits are unhappy and their ancestors are unhappy and their very nature is rebelling against this loss of connection to who they are. The educational facilities that have been set up in Africa are not teaching them the primal ways of African history and culture, but, instead they are being taught away from that. They are not being taught the power of their native language and the power of their primal spoken words and the guttural sounds that accompany the true pronunciation of the language that makes all the difference in the power of what is being spoken. They are not being taught to be proud, and to honor who they are, and where they came from, or about the great contribution that they have brought forward to humanity. They are being taught not to be Africans but to be European, American, English, etc, every thing except their own selves and race. They are being educated to make a way of life that does not involve who they are, but involves the false selves that they have been given and accepted.

There is nothing wrong with education, if it is truly education, in the right manner of approach. There is nothing wrong with being educated about other people and cultures, but not at the expense of denying your own. They should learn the foundation of themselves, and then seek other knowledge in the world, so that it can be checked, with checks and balances of their primal power and wisdom, that will not allow them to stray away from who they are. You can have the nice material possessions, but not at the expense of your heritage. Be educated in the trades and vocations, but be wise enough to know how far to go and not let it turn you against your self and your own nature. Use it as an accompaniment to your truth and way and better yourself with it. It does not matter how much you learn, nor how much education and success you attain, if it teaches you to not be who you are. This is totally against nature and is a true detriment to yourself. No learning is worth this. No learning is worth trying to be a natural, White person when you are a natural, Black person. No learning is worth anything, if it teaches you to hate yourself, to go against who you are. This is true for any race of people. Learn and share your culture and your knowledge, but always maintain who you are, for that is your identity of purpose, and that is what makes you who you are, in your own uniqueness.

What will Happen to the knowledge of our Ancestors

The knowledge of our Elders must be saved. It must be passed on and it must be passed on in its fullness. If not, then it becomes watered down and weak, and from generation to generation, less and less is passed on in fullness, until there isn't anything of real substance left. Since the youth of Africa is not taking advantage of what they have, the responsibility of this knowledge lies with the Africans living in America. When I say Africans living in America, I am speaking of the Black race that is called African Americans. The knowledge of our ancestors that is held by the African Elders must be brought forward to African American people in America. There is a growing interest among the Black African American people in their ancestors beyond the history of slavery. They are seeking it with a new enthusiasm and deep emotion that has them wanting, thirsting and hungry to reconnect with who they are. The Elders must be open to this and not be afraid to pass it on. If not, it will die with them. There are those Elders who are also caught up in the material possessions and pursuit of life. There are those who are selling their knowledge to other races and passing on culture and rituals. And the thing about it, is that some of them would rather pass it on to the White race, rather than their own Black American people, because they can pay for it, because they feel more comfortable passing it on to other races, because they have been mentally damaged themselves, particularly not to think of their own people. Some of them look at the Black American as not worthy enough and this perception must change.

    The other races can learn this knowledge but it will not be the same because it is not a natural, inherited, primal essence with them. They cannot possibly hold and maintain the essence in the same way a Black African person can. It is naturally, genetically, cellularly in the makeup of a Black person's DNA, racial memories etc. This is not to judge, or say that other races cannot share in this knowledge, but they are not the source of this knowledge and the natural, primal force that oozes through the blood of the African people. It does not have to be learned by the African people. It is the African people. The Elders need to be able to use their vision and ritual to know that there are those Black African Americans that should have this knowledge passed on to them because, if not, it will not survive. They have to be wise enough to see this, and understand this, and accept this. This is where the mantle of knowledge is moving, to the African American. This is their destiny.

The Africans living in America since slavery have been so disconnected and it so obscure as to who they are. For over 400 years through the process of natural evolution, natural selection, if you will, they are unfolding within, to the call of the ancestors from the spiritual dimensions, to reclaim who they are. And to take this knowledge, with the knowledge and growth attained from our experience in America, to another level of wisdom that is unsurpassed.

The Spirits Of The Elders Feel The Need To Teach

The elders are saddened by the fact that their youth are not growing into this knowledge and accepting that which must be passed on. They know that for the survival of this culture and heritage, they have to look outside of their immediate children. I say immediate children who are born in Africa but it must be understood that we are all children of Africa, we are all children of the Elders and we must be looked at and accepted as such. The future of this knowledge lies with the African American people and you will find that there are many of our ancestors who are now present interacting and inspiring African people in America to go to their roots and get the knowledge. They are being inspired to learn the true ways of themselves and to pass it on to their children. It cannot remain confined to the continent of Africa any more, for it must be allowed to flourish to Black African people the world over.

I myself have many African Ancestors and Ascended Masters with me, teaching me and guiding me, including a very powerful Council of African Ancestors numbering 12. These Councils and Ancestors are telling the Elders, in no uncertain terms, that they must pass this teaching on, but some are still caught up into thinking it is only to their immediate families. There are those who still do not trust the Black African American enough to pass it on. Many of them want to put you through many years of testing to see if you are worthy but yet will give it up to others without question. But understand that if the Elders use their abilities of ritual and ceremony and speak with the ancestors, they will know who to give the knowledge to and who not to. I do understand that they must be careful but, still, they know how to look into the heart of the recipient and know their intentions. The Elders are hurting but must accept the change that is being brought forward. It was meant to be this way and was never meant to be limited to only the continent of Africa born people. It is universal wisdom owned by no one but the custodians of a race of people who took the charge to use it to help elevate humanity on this Earth. The sooner the Elders can open up to this truth and confirm this with the Ancestors around them, the better it will be for the African people the world over. The Elders want to teach this so very badly to where it is painful to them to not be doing it. But many of them are looking with tunnel vision in one area, instead of the world community of African people, and there are many of them who are ready and ready now. Not years of testing, but now. Not a long drawn out period of preparation, but now.

There are a certain number of African American people who have been prepared before even being born into the physical world. They are opening up to an awareness that they were even unaware that they had. It is the timing and frequency of what is taking place in Creation, as we all go back toward the Oneness of All Things. We are all moving away from separation into unity from differences to sameness. We will not survive as a humanity if things do not change globally as a people of humanity. I know that there are those Black African people who will not agree with what I stated here but that is not my concern. I am fulfilling divine intentions and following the wisdom of those who work with me, of the Ancestors who are wise enough to know that things must change. They are not to be the way we think they should be, but should be the way God knows and the way that God knows is beyond our consciousness, unless we are united in oneness with God. Many of the decision that many

Black African people, who are knowledgeable and aware are being made with emotional attachments and hurt and even with the idea of revenge. It is understood but this does not make it right. You cannot rise above the lies, if you live the lies. You cannot rise above and beyond the falsehoods of what was done to the African people by being and doing the same as those who did it to us. I am not talking this, turn the other cheek garbage nor being this little passive person who will accept what ever is done to him. Don't get me wrong by what I said above. What I said above has more power than a physical beating or the returning of hatred and revenge can ever have.

So don't go around talking negative about what I said, because you truly don't understand what I said. If you take this attitude, believe me I will be the first to set people straight. I am speaking from a higher truth that cannot be grasp when you are in full of hatred and revenge because you absolutely become blind and stupid. You are smarter than that so, therefore, use your wisdom, to bring the justice that you seek, from a higher perspective.

Chapter 13
The Detriment of Religion To The Black Race

The Subject Of Religion

Well now we have done it! We have touched on a subject that so many people hold sacred and dear, the subject of religion. People are finding it very difficult to accept someone who speaks openly and honestly about their views and why they view it in the way they do. People look at you and judge you because a person may speak what they feel. "It is a blasphemy" they call out, and they point the finger at you with scorn and judgment and speak the wrath of God upon you. Well, if you want to know the truth, look at the state of affairs concerning religion today. Look at what is being done in the name of religion. Look at what it has done to the people. My focus is on the Black race and how religion has been very detrimental to it, and what need to be done to undo the damage that it has caused. We will go back to Africa before slavery and religion came into the Black peoples focus. Prior to the Caucasian race coming to Africa to inflict the cruelty of slavery and religion upon the African people, religion did not exist. They knew nothing about religion.

Blacks In Africa Did Not Have Religion

They paid homage and respect to the Mother Earth and Father Sky for the life that it gave to all who lived upon the Earth and under the Sun. They did not have the programming of religion to warp their minds and thinking processes, causing them to become mental slaves. Let me be sure that we clear up something before the judgment starts. I am speaking of a time long before the separation came among the people of Africa. I am speaking of a time when they lived in oneness and peace, brotherhood and sisterhood and did not have the conflicted minds of programmed religions. People do not want to accept that religions have been tampered with and changed and utilized for the good of those in control. But it was and still is being used as a device for control.

Now, even when the separation did set in among the people of Africa, there still were not the religions, even though they had different beliefs and cultures. There were those who even learned to understand the different ways of different tribes. Then the Europeans came in and added their tactics of separation and began to bring and force their religions among and upon the people in Africa because their way was considered savage by the messed up and ignorant thinking of the Whites who came to suppress and repress. Now we know that it wasn't all Whites who did this, so lets be clear about all this. I are not attempting judgment of anyone but only bringing forward the awareness and truth. When the Black people were taken into slavery to America and other lands, but particularly America, the bible was forced upon the slaves and this was the only allowed reading.

The Bible Was Allowed

Now, this did not happen right away. It was not allowed for them to read anything for a long time until someone realized the affect that teaching and allowing them to read the Bible would have on their minds. The oppressors knew this would kill their freedom of mind and thought. They knew if they could get them to become good Christians, they would be easy to control. It would not be necessary to worry about them because they would become mental and spiritual slaves, the good niggers. The Black people have been taught out of their cultures, beliefs, and natural ways of life, their spirituality, their freedom of thought and even how they viewed and understood God. They, the Black Africans, did not see and view God the same as the White race did. The Black people did not refer to the Supreme Being or the Great Source as God. For they did not use that word, They did not know that word. But they were taught so much misinformation by being whipped, chained and murdered into accepting this religion. They were frightened completely out of their culture, their natural way of praise and worship. Now, why would someone want to hold onto, and believe and accept, a religion that beat them into this unnatural way of acceptance? A religion that enslaved them and murdered them for many, many generations until their own beliefs were beaten, and bred out of them. How sick is this? How messed up does a mind have to be, to love and accept something as a way of life, as being Holy and of God, that did such tragic and horrible things to people their children, their parents and so forth? You really have to be mentally unstable, and basically seriously damaged to embrace this religion that was forced upon you during slavery.

This was not and is not the natural way or beliefs of the Black people. This, turn the other cheek concept, was interpreted for the Black slaves to make them obedient, to make them accept the slave master's whippings, and beating the stuffing out of them and their children. Forgive them for they know not what they do. Of course they knew exactly what they were doing. They knew that they were whipping your ass, they knew that they were killing you, raping you, your mother, your son and your daughter. Yes, they raped the boys as well.

Do Not Get Angry

Now let me stop here again for a moment so who ever is reading this is not getting in a bad state of mind. What is being spoken here is truth. It will make you free of all this anger, this hatred, this damage done by what happened to the Black ancestors, so the healing can begin. This truth affects Whites as well as Blacks. They are not immune to this. But this is not intended to bring up negativity, to get people up in arms. It should, and is being brought forth, so that the light of truth can be shed on it, and the world, and I mean all humanity, can look at it for what it was and is. Then as a people of humanity, change this and bring the releasing and the healing of this great pain and burden that is still carried by both Black and White.

People actually believe that going to church will truly cleans them of their so called sins, that it will make them acceptable to God, so they can go to heaven. This will not make it right. What will make it right is what you do personally, first to clear yourself, and then what we as humanity do collectively. The reason I say that religion is a detriment to Black people, and the same applies to all races, is that it does not focus on the aspects that can bring people into oneness and not separation, and it focuses on the aspect that is the letter of religion not the spirit of religion. There is an aspect to all religions that is beneficial to some degree. This aspect, of which I speak, is the mystical, metaphysical esoteric, spiritual. Many are confused as to what is spiritual in religion and what is metaphysical. There is much fear that has been put forth to keep one from going into the deeper aspects of religious study. If you really understand and go into the deeper aspects, then you will no longer see people as different in the ways that causes separation. You will no longer say that your religion is the only true religion and you will no longer be confused about the truth that is at the root of all religions. But, the religious practices today are about fear and shame and judgment and punishment if you don't follow their prescribed way.

Religion is supposed to take you to the point of no longer needing religion to define you or to give you the comfort needed to know that you are a part of God, or a Greater Energy or what ever you wish to call All That Is. Black people are so deeply and emotionally connected to their belief systems in religion, that for the most part, we are stuck in a way that has bound and fastened us together in and to a limited view. There is no room for expansion of awareness. We go too far with it and get lost and cannot find our way back. The Black race need to realize that we were given religion or should I say, religion was forced upon us. It is something that was, and is, not natural to our spirits and souls.

We were open and unlimited in our view of the Creator of All Things and did not look at the next tribe of people as being those who followed the wrong God or Way. We knew that every people and tribe had their cultures that led them to the Oneness and We, in fact, shared and learned from others, their ways and integrated them into what ever way we were practicing. It enhanced us, not destroyed us, like religion has done. Religion has shut us down and turned us away from the Oneness. It has robbed us of our freedom to share and learn and express. It has hurt us dramatically, and yet as a people we continue to hold on for dear life to something that we were beat into accepting. Something is really wrong with this picture.

Chapter 14
Gurhan from Andromeda and the Galactic Council

Greetings, I am Gurhan and I am from the Andromeda galaxy and I also sit on the Galactic Council of the Andromeda Galaxy. There is within the Andromedan system five thousand known solar systems with higher beings existing within them. There are approximately 250 ascended planets within the Andromedan galaxy and there are approximately five planets there that are similar to Earth with the size, shape and form of Earth. Some of these planets are being used to in the third dimension as places to transfer those who are on Earth who are not progressing or need to go to another system for certain soul lessons. There are certain soul groups that want to be with others like themselves.

The Black People are tied into the Mushaba Force, the Black People are tied into the Andromeda Galaxy, and the original codes that were brought to this planet. They were actually coming from another galaxy and came into this galaxy and then they were downloaded into Sirius and were downloaded into the Pleiades and there were other beings on Lyra so that there was a great deal of interventions. I would like to say from our perspective that the Black People are like the Fathers of the genetic morph structure of this planet and that they were the first physical form that was on earth. This means that Adam was more of the Black skin and even Moses and Jesus and many of the others were of the darker skin. It was the involvement of the lighter skin that came afterwards. So I believe that the darker skin people were the primordial people who carried the primordial codes and having done that they have a deeper connection to the Earth and a deeper connection to the galaxy and a deeper connection to the core energy, the core energy of all. But you and I both know that many of the Black People have lost this connection. This is why it is a part of what you are doing to reawaken the Black People on this planet to their connections.

The central core belief and the central core ideal of the Andromeda higher beings are often referred to as the Blue People but they have other names and there are other manifestations of them. Now I will tell you also that the Mushaba Force is a force that is also overcoming the polar opposites and the polarizations because it is a force that is the unity force. The unity force is that force which does not need to separate but to get into the fifth dimension requires the spiritual understanding that one can accept the left and the right, one can accept the hard and the soft and the unity of that and the unity of that then becomes part of the unification energy and your being then is allowed to exist in a state of actual manifestation of the fifth dimension which is a form but it is not a form like the third dimension

The fifth dimension puts you closer to the sixth dimension, which is where I am, where the Blue people are and the sixth dimension is closer to the Mushaba Energy which is the foundation for not only the people on this Earth but it is the foundation for people on other planets within the planetary system of the force of the Andromeda galaxy.

Ascended Masters of Color - Ascended Beings of Light

You are on a mission now that was explained to you perhaps two to three years ago where you are going to become a great teacher and you are going to be working on a more global level and you are going to bring forth energy for the Native people and the Black People and also introducing the concepts of color and how color relates to energy, how energy relates to thought and how color and energy relates to emotions and it goes on my dear friend.

Let me just say that remember that when I said there is an awareness that is beyond body so that if you put your awareness into a spiral and you become spiral energy and you become spiral consciousness and then you become a spiral being. Being a spiral being kind of like what you see in your DNA structure. Now what is it like to be in a spiral energy field? The spiral energy field is a unique energy that goes into other dimensions. So if you are working with the Mushaba Force and it is spiral energy, you can put yourself into a spiral energy field and you can do that now as I am speaking. You can even be able to even spiral in and out of other dimensions. This is the basis of string theory and string theory is an attempt by unified field physicist to explain the overall energy and how the energy works in the entire universe and these strings are postulated to be shaped as spirals. The spiral is the basic shape and this is what you need to know to go in and out of dimension. To go in and out of dimension you have to spiral and you know that it is a fact that when you ascend you going to be spiraling your energy upwards. The spiral of the Mushaba Energy is an energy that spirals in and out of other dimensions and can connect with other universes and I think you are already aware of that. The Mushaba Force energy in its spiraling does enable one to go not only in other dimension but other universes. To be able to do that requires a consciousness and awareness and a beingness and a presence.

There are people who are living in the violet energy field, St. Germain for example is of the violet flame and there are also the Andromeda energies of the Blue People and there is also people that are living in the golden white energy and there are also people living in the violet and as we said in the beginning there are people living in the black energy and we know you are interested in the black energy. It is not a black that is the black on earth because black on earth is defined as all the things without color, anything without color then becomes black. But this is an illusion and it is not a correct interpretation of black.

The black that you see on Earth is without color but there is a black that is not without color but it is a color. I have a difficult time using Earth terminology to describe this because it does not make any sense. How can it be a color but without color? Let me say that there is a beauty when you look at the sky and see this blue it is a deep blue and it is a blue that is indescribable especially when the blue sky is lit with sunlight. Now imagine that you look at the space and we look at the galaxies, we look at the universes, and we look at the different stars and we see this black out there but that black is actually a color it is not without color. You know and your scientist knows that the space that is defined as black is actually filled with energy and it is even a name for it which is dark matter. So that is an attempt to

Ascended Masters of Color - Ascended Beings of Light

describe this. The colors and the states of awareness are producing the state of being so that if you combined the state of being with a form and in this case a spiral form, then you can move in and out of dimensions.

The midnight black energy is an energy of inter-universes and the midnight black is also an energy of creating the links between the universes. The soft pink with brilliant spirals of purple is an energy of the inter-dimensions. Now I would like to say to you and I think that you have understood this, is that this energy called the Mushaba is an energy that connects universes not just dimensions but universes and the connecting of the universes is something that the Earth is not ready to deal with because they already have problems accepting dimensions. Now we are going to say that there are different universes and some of the scientist does know that. Now the midnight black energy is the energy of the creative force which began the big bang and that there was a midnight black energy that was going through and still is part of the expansion of the universe. The other energy the soft pint with purple spirals is the energy that is linked to holding the energy field within the galaxy, here within the universe itself. So you have two methods of using this Mushaba Force.

Chapter 15
An Entity Called Nigger

This Word Is Being Fed

This word carries far too much power. It is a word, a compilation of 6 letters that was given meaning by a man that alluded to a description of a people. This description was meant to be degrading and low and dirty and psychologically damaging. It was given a very bad energy around and through it. It was brought to life by a people, who created it and constantly spoke it, with rage, passion, anger, judgment and hatred. It became an entity that hung over the Black race for over 400 years and is still there. It has been fed constantly by racial separation and judgments. One of the things that is most powerful is that it is being kept alive by the Black race itself. The Black people have adopted and accepted this man made nigger entity as their own. It was welcomed to the race of Black people after there was so much dislike, hatred and the word was so despised. Black people have been so beat up and murdered with that word to where the Black race became numb to it. Now it is accepted and used by many, far too many Blacks particularly, the younger people and it has even spread to being used among young Whites and other races as an acceptable word of expression. It is even lovingly and affectionately used among many Black people. Many Blacks feel it is ok. for them to call each other nigger.

But it is not alright and the truth of this is that if Whites or other races call a Black person nigger, it will most likely be a serious consequence behind it. It is still being glorified in movies and music. Yet, there is another element among the Black race that still hates the word and is trying very hard to stop the use of it. It has become a culture of its own. The entity has grown into its own accepted culture. Now, none of these are good. Those who accept it as described above, and those who do not accept it, as described above. Either way it is still being fed and kept alive because it is still feeding off the people and the life giving energy that they are giving it. This is a part of our history, says many Blacks and, in one sense, this is true. But, it is not who we are and we should not accept this as who we are. Now let us look at the various reasons why it is so powerful today even more than it was during the time of slavery.

This word is being accepted as good among youth

What a skillful, masterful job done on the Black people and on the youth in particular. This word, this living entity, called nigger reached further and wider than was ever imagined. The idea was to degrade, belittle, insult, mentally damage etc. It was successful in so many ways. What is happening now with the youth, is that they are accepting it and including it as a part of who they are. What is happening is that the youth think they have taken the steam and the hatred out of it. In one sense, maybe so, but not in another. They have taken the degrading, belittling affect away from it to a degree, and the insult to them personally as well. At least this is how they see it. But there is something that is underlying that many people don't understand and we will get to that in a moment.

Let us take a closer look at how the power of this entity works.

The youth have taken a bad, negative word in its use and turned it around to an acceptable good word in use among themselves and among certain other young people of different races. Things that are said like" That's my nigger, Hey nigger what's up, Nigger you know how I feel about you, we homies, we boys, Nigger you the best thing that ever happened to me, I don't know what I would do without my nigger, Us niggers have to stick together, etc. And it doesn't matter if it is said differently, for instance "nigga". You get the picture. Many of these words are said with a great deal of affection and reverence. It is accepted as being alright. But let a White youth say to you "this is my nigger" or any race youth say that, and they are ready to be beat or killed for using that word toward someone who call each other nigger all day long. Now there are a few, a very few Whites and other race youth, who are so close with certain Blacks that they calls each other nigger, because among them it is an accepted culture. But if another Black who hears it and is not with that particularly vibe, then that opens the door to more anger and separation. Because one might say: "Nigger what's wrong with you letting that white boy call you nigger! You crazy or something, what's up with that nigger!" And then an argument or fight could ensue that could lead to a number of outcomes.

Now the young Whites and youth of other races are also affected. Nowadays, White youth and others are calling each other nigger! That's right I hear White youth saying the same thing to each other" what's up nigger, nigger please etc. So now they are damaged as well. I will get back to showing why none of this is good and why I say people are damaged by it.

Those Who Hate This Word

Now let's take a look at the other percentage of Blacks, particularly, the older Blacks, the educated Blacks, the Blacks who are very religious and Blacks who have great pride and just don't care for that word. Now this percentage keeps this word alive because they have such hatred for the word. This entity is being fed energy, whether it is affection or hatred, it is being given energy and it does not care what kind of energy it receives, as long as it is being fed and kept alive. Some people get so angry when they hear the word, and extra angry, when they hear it used by a White person. There have been all kinds of forums on the word and all kinds of action on the word and yet it still remains powerful. It is one of the most powerful words in the history of this country because it has so many rippling effects in so many, many ways.

Then you have the entertainment industry. This medium is all powerful. This word is used so loosely in film and music, particularly that which is called Black music, hip hop, rap and the movies that are called Black movies. I am not talking about films made about the history of slavery that use the word, because it is a part of what it was during that period and it is an education of how it all began with the use of the word that became an entity. This is history, the past and it should be left there, as a reflection to look back on, for growth and expansion, and evolvement of the minds of men and women all across the globe. Unless things change, before long you might see aliens flying around the galaxy calling each other nigger, "nigger, get your space ship out of my way etc. Get the picture.

This Word Damages Black And White

Alright, how do we bring the power of this entity down? First, let me explain why I say it has damaging affects on not only Black people but Whites and others as well. The use of the word, in any sense, is no good. The N word itself, which has become a massive sort of living entity, carries a history that is dark, and a history that is full of murder, hatred, separation, and rape, a history that is negative in action and deed. When it is being used in any form, it is being kept alive, to keep pushing out from itself the dark energies that it represents. It actually releases these powerful living thought forms. And what is not understood, is that these thought forms become fed and so powerful themselves that they become entities, separate from, but connected to the massive entity called nigger. Thought forms affect people very powerfully and they have no clue. Thought forms draw to them the same family and like energies that resonate with them and what they represent, very powerfully. And the entity, the word nigger, still powerfully represents darkness, separation, and hatred,. and it is being kept alive to continue to grow and grow and create more and more of this negative energy. The problem is that many do not understand this and think that it is alright because they are not doing or saying anything negative.

Why would you love something that represents murder, hatred, lies and separation? Why would you hate something that represents all the above? You are either feeding this entity with love of it, or hatred of it, and either way it is living off what it is being given. You may say, "well it is living off of the love I give it, isn't that good?" What is good about keeping and loving something that represents a dark history? Why keep it alive with hatred? The power of this entity has infiltrated the minds of people to such an extent that the thinking and mind processes when it comes to this word, are warped, very warped. Sending love energy with the Light and the Divine Love of God or Creation, toward healing something is powerful. But the love of something dark that was created by man's thought, is not serving to dissipate this energy, but helping it to remain. Do you see the difference in the love I speak about?

This Word Needs To Be Put To Rest

This entity, this word, this energy called nigger needs to be put to rest once and for all. Not the history of it as a lesson, but the continued use of it, the continued glorifying of it, the continued feeding it hatred and love, of the darkness in it, and it needs to be laid to rest. The power of it has people so confused that they don't see the harm in keeping something this dark alive. It is still a ticking time bomb among people and it is a word that people have to walk on egg shells around and be so very, very careful of. It causes so much tension, friction and misunderstanding. What is good about all that? This should be seen for what it is. It represents something too big and too powerful for humanity to allow it to live among us. It's the same with any words or entities of darkness. People have lost jobs behind it, had their lives and careers ruined behind it, and many people

White and Black keep it alive to continue to be used as a weapon against understanding and unity. It is a weapon of darkness, of hatred, and of separation.

If you as a Black person do not wish to be called nigger by Whites or any other race or by your own race then stop it by starting with yourself. Stop calling yourself nigger. Stop accepting this as a culture as how you define yourself. I heard a Black youth say that White people have not earned the right to use the word nigger or call Black people nigger. How sick is this statement? How in the hell does anyone earn the right to call you something as dark as nigger. It was certain White people who created the word, gave it life and created an entity out of it. So, how can you say they don't have a right to use it, when they are the creators of it? Those same certain White people gave it to you to use on yourselves and you gladly own the word as your own. They also gave it to other Whites to use on Blacks as well and in their ignorance they gladly accepted it. Neither they, nor anyone should have the right to use that word anymore. It should be the law of the people of humanity that says no! no more! This word, this entity is dead. It is not allowed! When will we wake up and realize that the spoken word has great power? It does create! It does affect people's minds, thoughts and feelings.

This Word causes Hatred And Separation

The use of this word carries a strong and powerful vibration that shakes the very foundation of hatred and separation. It is felt by many and this is what brings up the anger in so many. It also, for Whites, brings up anger because it carries a strong, powerful vibration of guilt by association. This guilt feeling causes anger in those who really don't like the word and feel that they should not be held responsible for what a certain group of Whites have done. Whether they are ancestors or not, they feel the guilt of this word. They feel that "because I am White Blacks feel I am responsible, that I am to blame" and this is not right either. We as a people, and I am speaking about all people as humanity, better begin to look at it for what it truly represents and begin to dismantle the power of this word, this entity called nigger. The word nigger is a program. It is a program that brings up much hatred and fear and many, many feelings among Black and White. People are programmed to react to that word whenever they hear it. Pay closer attention to what goes on within you, especially to what you feel when it is being said by different people and you will get different programmed reactions. What will you do about the use of this word, nigger? That is a question you have to answer within your self.

Chapter 16
The First And The Seventh Ray Energy

We will speak about the first and seventh ray energies to help bring a little clarity about what they mean.

The First Ray

The first ray is the ray of God's Will. It is the ray of power and it is the ray of faith. It carries with it various attributes, such as truthfulness, courage, strength, dedication and steadfastness. What does all this mean in terms of how it relates to the Black people who are people of the first ray? This first ray energy flows through the Black race as a natural by-product of it's existence. This is not to say that people of other races can not achieve this ray. This is saying that it is naturally inherent in Black people. They can achieve the other rays, as well, which comes naturally to certain other races. The ray of power depicts the strength of Black people and the internal power that they carry. They are truly, without doubt, and you see that even today, Black people are people of faith and of God's Will and through the flames of creation the Black race have breathed forth great beams of the first ray of God. Black people were to set an example as to how to use the qualities of this ray with love, wisdom, understanding and compassion. It was important to use the power of this ray to overcome illusion and adversity, which the Black race have suffered with tremendously.

There were others, as well, but our subject matter is on the Black race.

Black people had to have incredible faith in order to have endured what they did for over 400 years. They had to have faith that it must have been God's will, in order to give them the power and faith and strength to go on. This first ray energy, mastered by any one, regardless of race, because is not about race, has accomplished something very profound. To carry and use this first ray energy is something that all of us in humanity must master. Living and doing and being God's Will, having undeniable faith, and realizing the great power that one carries is a part of the evolution of humanity. In fact, mastering all the qualities of all the rays is necessary for mastery and completion. But it is only being referenced to Black people, because of the subject at hand, and how it relates to the Black race and their mission, and what gives them the courage and the strength, the faith and the power to continue, regardless to how difficult or extremely harsh the conditions are. This is what this first ray energy will do for any person who masters these qualities. It was necessary to be a foundation for the Black race because of what they chose to play out in the world of humanity.

The first ray represents the alpha, the beginning, and that relates to the information provided in this book about the Black people being the beginning of the race of man on this Earth and the contribution of the Black genetics to bring together what we now know as the Adam species or human on this Earth.

The Seventh Ray

The Black people are also people of the seventh ray. This seventh ray energy represents freedom, justice and absolute victory and mercy. And the Black race has been fighting and struggling for freedom for a long, long time. They have been struggling for justice, victory, mercy and redemption for a very long time. This ray is inherent, as well and this is why the Black people are fighting so hard for true freedom and victory. They are fighting for justice and mercy so they can be free and empowered! This ray is also the ray of purification and transmutation which are qualities of this violet flame ray. The seventh ray is the omega, the end. The rays together represents the beginning and the end. It begins with Black people and it will end with Black people.

But realize, we are speaking on a deeper, spiritual vibration and this is not to be taken in egotistical, material terms. The rays combined, mean a people who are about God's will, power and faith and a people of freedom, justice, victory and mercy. They are a just people. With all that has been done, there is still mercy for all people, there is still justice brought forward. Black people want to see all people free. There is so much to be said about the combination of the first and seventh rays and why it was necessary for them to be naturally inherent in the Black race. Without it, the Black race would not have survived all that they endured to this day.

Chapter 17
Djwhal Khul's Message To Anakhanda

Your Strong Sense Of Love

Good afternoon, and greetings to your most Divine Heart and It is I Djwhal khul who sits with you now. There are questions and we will answer them in one voice. But more than that, there is the need of this hour to share with you, that your essence, that which you are, the light that you are, is gathering the speed at this time and twirling and swirling and spiraling into a very brilliant new ascended time and presence upon your planet. I wish to take my hat off to you and to bow before you. For you are persistent and you are consistent, and you are deep within the heart in your desire to come forth in mastery, and to flower and to bloom as the energy, and as the individual, and the united one, and the uniting one, that your are.

In my eyes, this day, there are tears. They are tears of gladness, not of sadness, tears of friendship, I have been watching you and am most pleased with your growth and with your strong sense of love. I, as Djwhal Khul, have had an interest, oh yes, in your development, and so have many others. Watching you educate yourself and wake yourself up, even as others have come in the night, and in the day, and in the softness of twilight, in the times between the times when the mind is more still and less is going on all around you. And we have come with a message, with a murmur, with a whisper, with a vibration, with a wave form, to simply carry to you, on a wave length a little spark, to allow the spark of the Holy God within you to simply brighten a bit, to glisten a bit, to wake up one way. And you have responded to many sparks and there will be others who will respond to you. So I bow before you, as a Spark of God, as one who carries the signature of the energy of Creator and of God. But you are not alone for that spark is within all and so it is very mighty and very wonderful and yet it is what belongs to every form of life. In this, you are one with your sister and your brothers wherever they are. And yet, your choice to wake yourself up, to really pull the sleep out of your eyes, and expand your heart, has been noted and because of that you shall move more smoothly, perhaps, into the time of the ending of time.

Many of your questions apply to what is called your past. It is interesting to try to piece together the past, is it not? To try to determine why this thing has happened and why that thing has happened and what was this and what was that.

Time

But I want to tell you something about time. It is a form of energy and that which is your past and that which is your future are side by side and that which is your present exists also in the same time frame. And in one sense, it is all a part of the same energy it is not easily explainable or describable or definable, oh no! And yet, this energy of time shall come to be something that you do understand So it is interesting that you look to the past, when in one way it would befit you to look to the present, to look into the present moment, for in one more instance, it becomes your past.

It is coming to that time when it would be appropriate for you to live in the present moment even though the mind wants to understand the past. How interesting, How curious, is it not? And you might say, but if I am to live in the present moment then I will not get my questions answered about the past. Yet you will. For all relevant knowledge and all important information and all matters of importance are coming to be made known to you.

The Transference To The New Earth

The Heavens are beginning to open up and in the transference to the New Earth, you shall rediscover that which was once known, and then forgotten, and such memory shall return softly and intimately and all the pieces of all the puzzles will begin to line up, join hands and come to be reinserted into what you would call your consciousness, your memory banks. For nothing has ever been lost, only separated for a time, for were it not for this particular time on this particular Planet with the forgetting, then you would not have had the objective that all of you have. Upon the revelation of memory, the landscape would have changed and it would not have been possible to pursue a certain line of living. And now, that line, that discovery, that whole pilgrimage into the unfolding of present Earth is about to come to a very wonderful climax.

As you prepare with all the others to transcend and ascend your soul into the next level of Creation, then it will be time to reinsert, you might say, those disks of lost data and more things will come back on line, as you come back on line. Greater understanding will be yours.

All this in good time, I say, and all this in the proper timing Let me say that those who work with energies and force, and qualities that are way beyond what you now know, with them in a certain intimate relationship with the energy, and the form of energy, that you call time.

And so, there is an appropriateness to a return of knowledge and there is an appropriateness to a yearning for knowledge and all things line up into an absolute beautiful pattern that is called evolution, and that is called manifestation.

All Around You Is About To Shift

And it all moves according to a certain rule and I would dare to say now, that the entire structure of how things have been in your body, in your Earth and all around you is about to shift quite dramatically. So that what has been a structure, will be restructured and what has been an energy, will be reenergized, what has been a connection, will become a reconnection, what has become a balance will, become a new balance, and what has been a separation, will transcend into unity. Is Djwhal talking in symbols? Is Djwhal talking in riddles? Oh no! What I am doing, is heralding in the new time, the New Earth, the new energies, and the new purpose. For soon it shall be revealed to you, just who you are and why you are here. Until this point, there were many reasons for your purpose and many reasons for your life on Earth. And yet, the total purpose has not been revealed to you nor can it be revealed by one such as myself or any other.

And why is that? Are we unkind to you, in that we do not answer your questions appropriately or fully? Oh no! It is because you are coming back on line and we would never rob you of the joy of self-discovery. It has a little link to self mastery and it has a little link to knowledge of the Self, which will reveal who and what you are and why you are here. When you know this, then it won't take long before you are catapulted into the right position for everything to happen that you have chosen to be a part of, prior to this birth. Until then it is a matter of piecing what you can together, balancing what you can, keeping the heart open, reaching for love and deepening the experience, holding the hope that Gabriel brings.

Gabriel's Involvement

Let us talk about your questions. In your first question, you mention Gabriel's position, and you want to know "what is Gabriel's extent of involvement with you in bringing forward certain information? Let us say, that the extent of Gabriel in bringing forth information to you depends upon the extent of openness and understanding and receptivity that you possess. It is not simply that Gabriel will carry and convey to you all messages, bring to you all acknowledgements and carry and convey to you all proper intonations and vibrations, not always in words, but to bring forth yourself into the next realm or room. It is your energy that seeks out such information and then draws it forth. It is always a give and a take, it is always that, as you take in from Gabriel, it is equal to the extent that you are prepared to give out to others. And the extent that you are prepared to give out to others is quite noted by the Councils and so we bow in reverence to you.

You are one who wishes to give, therefore, your capacity to receive will equal that capacity to give. However, you may stand forth and say, well I am ready to receive everything and I am ready to give everything and it is quiet a gesture and it is a strong statement of exclamation that you might deem as very true. But the truth of that statement, comes in and within, the Divine timing of the unfoldment of the energy unit of that which you are. So I would say, that sometimes you are ahead of yourself and sometime you are behind yourself in that which you think you are. And yet, it will all catch up and come together.

Information Comes In The Form Of Knowledge

Information comes in the form of knowledge, it comes in the form of knowledge that is open and available, and it comes in the form of knowledge that is hidden and more secretive. When the mind and the body and the soul and the spirit are lined up in perfect unity and order, then the current of information that is energetic, and that has a signature and has a vibration, can then be sent forth and can acclimate through each of those parts of you. You are spirit. You also have what is called the soul which is connected into the Divine Energy, into the body that you possess and you have a spirit energy that is beyond that.

You also have that mental energy of openness or choice to close down on a certain belief or truth, to hold it into words, to hold it into something that it is not. It is almost as if an ocean of information is being brought now to the consciousness of humanity and they wish to hold that ocean in a fish bowl. And you can't hold it, well, maybe a part of it and that is fine, but all of it will not fit. For there is no language for the Love that is Eternal and there is no explanation of the knowledge that is vibration. Knowledge is essence. It is vibration and it changes you from the inside to the outside. There is no way for me to answer to the extent of involvement that you would have with one such as Gabriel, for it will change, depending upon you and depending on how fast your world receives. Right now, your world is moving very quickly. It is fast forwarding into the ascension frequencies. The more love, the fewer ideas, less thinking, and the more feeling, and the more Archangel Gabriel can come forth and bring messages to you.

Surrender to The essence of ultimate truth

The less inclined you are to hold the messages to a certain tenant, to a certain truth, to a certain doctrine, and allow them to come in like the language of light, light geometry, twirling and swirling in your atmosphere. Allow it to come into the heart softly and it shall come. The extent of involvement that you have with any Master or Angel depends upon your growth and evolution, depends upon your level of understanding and your ability to let go of beliefs and move into the surrender of the essence and purpose of Ultimate Truth. To allow yourself to bypass the smaller knowledge's and go into the crux of the matter, into the knowledge that is more fundamental, that is very holy. Much knowledge has been taught and then there is the knowledge that goes beyond that, beyond all of that, which I cannot talk about. And this knowledge and it's essence, comes in, in currents of energy.

So open the heart to that which is beyond understanding and then you stand under a current of energy that expands the mind, along with the heart, and it prepares you for safe passage and expanded evolution into the next moment, within present time, and these properties of growth take place in the now moment, in the present dawning of the moment. They do not take place in the reflection of what has been or what will be. For in those moments there is a thread of energy, like a tube that is stopped up by, what almost, lets say, cuts it off at the pass, you might say, because of the dwelling on the past. And you might say, but Djwhal, I want to know why certain things have happened and how will I know, if I do not have the information. Because right now it is like a patch work quilt with many squares that are not there, they're not colored in. But I assure you, Beloved One, the quilt will be restored.

El Moriya And Isis

I did, perhaps, talk about an ascended aspect of El Moriya. Perhaps I spoke about an ascended aspect of Isis. Do you know that you have ascended aspects of your Self, all in different levels, all carrying out different orders, holding different purposes, actuating different realities, originating in a slightly different frequency? Everyone has a certain individuality, you might say, in one level of reality and another in another level of reality. Let us simply say that, that energy of Isis has a counterpart in the energy of Mother Mary, in the Archangel of Mary and in other energies that have no names. There are aspects of the Isis energy that are walking upon the Earth now, aspects of El Moriya that sit within councils now and all those aspects are simply links of one line, one lineage you might say but even that lineage is connected to other lineages through those clusters of souls.

And so, I would want to say to you, that it is not necessary in one sense, that you have the names of ascended aspects of El Moriya and Isis that were in Black skin or White skin. In fact, Isis was in Black skin and, perhaps, you might say that El Moriya has always been of the darker skin. Oh yes he has on Earth! So, please, know something about skin color. No one is Black and no one is White, all races come from the Heart of God.

Blue and Violet Ray Races

When we have spoken about the blue color, the Blue race, the Violet race, and talked about it in terms of Black skin, people who have roots within the blue ray energy within the violet ray energy, we were speaking of ray energies. We were not saying that these Beings had violet skin or blue skin. It is more the ray quality that we were talking about. Perhaps you might say, well did their skin have a tinge of violet and did their skin have a tinge of blue and, perhaps, it is true. Perhaps, there is a little blue in black, perhaps there is a little violet in blue. But we are speaking more than that, about qualities of rays that you know about. Perhaps the skin has a tinge but it wasn't a violet race it was a violet ray race. What is the violet ray all about is it not about freedom? What is the blue race about is it not about love, will and power?

You might say that the Black race mastered frequencies that were about freedom, came here to deal with issues of power, issues of freedom. Very interesting, you might say, that there was a violet color in the aura, not really in the skin, more in the aura, more of a ray connection, more of a tone, a song, a vibration, not necessarily a skin color. It was the virtue that it was carrying. In this way, no one is Black or White but each essence carries a certain quality of a ray and all races come from the Heart of God, where in the rays come forth as essences. In one sense, you might say, that the White race was a little bit more aligned with the second ray of love of wisdom, of a certain purity, maybe you might say, that the Black race was a little more aligned with the first ray, issues of power, will and faith and the seventh ray and all. Maybe there were other races that were more aligned with the third ray aspect. Do you see what I mean? It is not exactly that it was a violet skin or a blue skin.

Lemurian Race

You said to me that the Lemurian race was the Blue and the Violet races that were called the Black race during the time of the high African civilization. What we are saying is that in the demise of Lemuria there were many scattered outpost. There were many scattered Beings, who have perhaps, escaped from the center of Lemuria. There was a Lemurian seed that was brought forth and the original seed of Lemuria came from many different places, all of them extraterrestrial. So you have planted into the heart of what was later to become Africa, some of the Lemurian seed. It isn't a history lesson so much that you are after, is it, But what is it that you are after? And I ask you this question really wanting to know. Because in Lemuria there were many Beings, and there were Beings that seeded a certain race, and actually many races were seeded.

Ascended Masters of Color - Ascended Beings of Light

The Violet race and the Blue race were those that carried the essences of the Blue and the Violet rays. Now, there has always been a little interesting kind of talk about the rays. In some aspects, the blue ray is the first ray. When you get further out into those colors, when you get close to the Earth, the first ray has been called the red ray. But the blue ray is the original force from beyond Earth and is considered the first ray, the ray of Archangel Michael, always seen in the sapphire blue. So those ray essences went into the make up of those races in Lemuria and many things happened and there were many who left in ships and there were many who brought themselves to other places to colonize other civilizations.

And when Lemuria was, well, when the upheaval came, Lemuria and Atlantis were in existence at the same time during one period of time and the seed, you might say, within those extraterrestrials who came to seed the planet was brought to various parts and various continents. Therefore, the Violet and the Blue race people, not skin, but people, were living in the African civilization, in that part of what you now call Africa. Now, during the time of Atlantis and Lemuria there were many outposts that you call extraterrestrial outposts all over the globe. Your world was very different then and it was a decision made at higher levels to create a world that was extremely diverse. On most planets, there is only one race, one people, with one sort of look, one sort of language, maybe two, but not the diversity that has been on the Earth. Earth has been a very interesting spot, a melting pot, in one sense. Many different lines of races brought about their virtues of rays to be seeded, or brought to live upon one planet in a remote part of one galaxy. It was for the simple reason for playing out a very unique purpose in the galaxy and in the universe. Therefore, great detail went into the seeding of the planet and the diversity of life upon the Earth.

You might say that everyone upon the Earth has an extraterrestrial origin, for many came, did they not, to bring that kind of diversity of life and allow it to spin evolution together and play out the different polarities and stories upon the surface of the Earth. At this time, all of those stories and all of that diversity is ending, and karma itself is ending, and what is happening on the Earth is the movement to the next level up, for everyone. Therefore, a sense of unity must now come forth, a oneness must now come forth, and that is the focus of the hour.

Blue And Violet Becomes Black

It is not really easy in one sense to explain how the Blue and the Violet races ended up being the Black race. It had to do with the skin and the sun and even the loss of one of the Earth's Moons which changed the atmosphere and changed the skin tone on the people. But, bare in mind, that they did not have violet skin or blue skin, it was more an auric color and a tone, a virtue. The very tall Africans and certain other Beings and races from Sirius, and from other places and star systems, all brought themselves into the continent of Africa. It was lush, and it was beautiful, so much life there. It was a very exciting continent. How did one race end up being a part of this race and that race?

Let us simply say that the seeds were thrown out on the field of diversity and there was migration of one tribe

Ascended Masters of Color - Ascended Beings of Light

and another tribe of one nation and another nation based upon similar needs based upon similarities, originalities, all of that, that brought together many races that then began to intermix and interbreed. You end up, with a race that in one sense lost some of its consciousness, because the Violet race and the Purple race as we call it, were living in a slightly higher frequency of vibration. Everyone on the Earth lowered their vibration as more and more dissent, more and more negativity, you might say, was introduced and followed within the experiment of the diversity on the Earth.

You might say, that there were many that came to the Earth with a slightly different agenda. Perhaps they had a planet that blew up, perhaps they came to find a dwelling upon the Earth, for it seemed like a place where many of diversity could gather. And maybe some of them came with a certain dignity of the light, and perhaps some of them came with a lesser dignity of the light and a little more of a gray quality. And perhaps there was a lowered consciousness, a decline and a different agenda. On the Earth there are many who are of the light and there are also many who are of a dimmer light. This has been part of the purpose on the Earth.

Free Will Zone

This entanglement, this sort of warring factions, this sort of a sense of following free will into a zone that is not exactly as God would choose first, is what all of the people on the Earth have begun to exercise, that which is free will and begin to test the waters so to speak. Sometime tempted by a darker race, and I don't mean skin color, I mean a race of beings that are more inclined toward a darker intent, toward what you might call, not the light side of the word, but the darker side of the word. I am not speaking of skin color here. I am speaking of more alignment with the light and alignment with a darker nature, see what I mean? And this sort of energy has always been played out on the Earth. What happened is that the free will zone has opened up and many made choices that brought down the consciousness on the Earth, which was once of a higher nature, and begun a system of time, to re-evolve towards the light. I would not say that a mistake was made, I would say that it might be looked at as an experiment in evolution, in consciousness, in unity. And I would say that the end of that experiment is at hand. It is not quite so easy to answer some of these questions because each one of the questions is like a whole chapter in history.

Slavery Did Not Originate On Earth

Now I wish to say, regarding the story about the Roman Catholic Priest coming up with the idea of slavery, I want to say that maybe that was true and maybe that was not true. But the truth that want to be given to you at this point, is simply this, the idea of slavery did not originate in Africa, not by a White race and not by other Black races for their were Black races that used other Black races as slaves. But the idea of slavery did not originate there, it did not originate on Earth. It was brought to the Earth. It is an idea based upon a lack of love, and a lack of light, and a misuse of power that was, and is, in the galaxy and in the universe. Therefore, what I am saying to you is that slavery is not a new thing. There are many worlds that had certain levels of slavery, other races, races that don't look anything like you, that are not even humanoid at all. The idea of misuse of power didn't originate on the Earth although the Earth has certainly perked up in that direction.

So it isn't really something that we can pin on a Roman Catholic Priest somewhere wearing a White skin. The idea of it comes from an abuse of power that has been around for a very long time and was passed along as a lower vibration. It comes from fear. The need to aggressively control someone else comes from a fear of running out, not having enough, from not having enough love. It comes from a dim experience of a lack of love and a lack of light. And there are worlds beyond worlds, and many focuses, and focal points, where that energy of light and dark, light versus dark has been played out in your local galaxy. So, it didn't originate here and I would like to take off some of the blame that may have been placed on the Roman Catholic Priest. Certainly there are many within the realms of religions that also entertain the idea of cruelty through control, even to the omission of truth, to the editing of Holy Scriptures and the persecution of those who do not line up with the churches ideas. So many forms of slavery exist, other than what you would call, the slavery of the Black race.

Andromeda

There have been many different races that have performed what you would call genetic experiments with the human species. Not all Andromedans are dark and have worked in a negative way with the genetics of human kind. Some have and some have not. There are many levels to every question, many, many levels. There are the Sirians that had the good nature of the human evolution as their best interest and there were others who came to usurp energy. Just as light and dark are played out upon the Earth, they are played out also in this galaxy and have been played out. Let us say that there is something very special about the human experiment on Earth and the position of the Earth and for that reason many, many races have wanted to control the human being on the Earth. Many races have wanted to control those living on the Earth. There is a specific position of the Earth in the galaxy that is very important, that I am not allowing myself to go into at this time. For that reason many have come to conquer the Earth and those that live upon it, to alter them, to create slaves, to create power structures, where they benefit and so on.

The good news is that the Earth has achieved the balance she needed to close out that scenario and now it is over, now it is what you call the end times. Because that period of history is over and Earth goes up to another level and Earth goes up to sing a new song, a song of freedom, a song of unity, and a song of love. And it ends those chapters and begins a new chapter. It begins such a new chapter that I would call it a new book altogether. The book of life that shall begin to be written upon the Earth is of a higher vibrational quality and all will change. Therefore, only harmony will be in the new realm and that is already existent. And you and you and you and everyone are helping to assist and create the focus of life that shall come to pass in that realm. So hold the heart open in deep love

Sirius

We are talking about Sirius A and the dolphin energy is a little more associated with the Sirius B energies. Let us simply say that there were Sirians who sent scouts to the earth and did some experiments, some not so good, some with the goodness in mind. Both sides of the Sirians has played out upon the Earth, the side that wanted to control, and the side that did not want to control. In fact, the story of control is one that has been played out very often on the Earth. The Sirians came and built outposts upon the Earth so that they can watch the Earth so that they can learn, so that they can teach, so that they can expand, so that they could watch the development. You might say that they are the higher, little older, brothers and sisters to the Earth. So there were the good Sirians, you might call it, and then you call it the not so good Sirians. Both of them playing parts, one to help, and maybe the other, to simply help themselves. All that can be imagined has been played out upon the Earth.

Lion Head Figure On The Sphinx

The pyramids were built through a process of Divine force that used levitation and that also employed dematerialization and materialization. The sphinx, if you look at it, looks like a cross, does it not, between a human and a lion. You see the paws, you see the lion head, do you not? Let me remind you that there are many, many races as diverse as you might have seen in movies such as Star Trek or Star Wars, very many races. And many of the races have the look of the lion. In fact, the lion energy is very strong and very divine. There are many cat like, feline, civilizations. The body of the sphinx itself is almost like a code and when you look at the face and the body of the sphinx, it is an energy that encodes a certain openness. It is like the crop circles, when you look at a crop circle, you may not understand all the dimensions and all the angels and circles, but what is being given to your consciousness, is a certain encodement to remember and it is the same with the sphinx. It is a hidden knowledge, a hidden memory, you might say, of a race, of a grand race, of a lion race and a human race coming together, of human and extraterrestrial, all working together, building these structures to hold memory, to hold knowledge. And at the very right time it will explode the gift and the inheritance of that knowledge.

Within the sphinx are spaces in physicality where much knowledge is hidden and may be revealed and discovered. But the sphinx itself is an encodement and has the potentiality and possibility of opening up the mind and the heart into transcendence. After all, the least that it does is tell humanity that they are not alone. The incredible mess of unjust and misadvised information, of withholding from the public the understanding of extraterrestrials, and the hiding of it and all of that, that is going on in your world. Certainly there are many who now know but certainly there are many who still think that they are the only life that exists and the Sphinx stands tall in the desert as a statue, as a monument to extraterrestrial and human existence

Those who died n Africa are seeding the new world

I would like to say that the Aids virus that was brought in and distributed in Africa, which certainly was an act of darkness, an act of treachery; but what I wish to say to you that many of the ones that have died from this tragic illness, this created illness you might say, are living now upon the new Earth. There is no death and certain people kind of got in the way of things and others choose to be the bearer's who would demonstrate to humanity what cannot be allowed to ever occur again. We want to say that many of the ones who died of this tragic illness were the ones who chose to reveal something that would stand out and be remembered. When something happens to many, it is remembered. When it happens to one, it is forgotten, and they knew this. Others kind of crossed signals and kind of ended up in death and it was not so much of a soul choice. But let me say that there is no death and let me say that many of those who have recently passed are now living upon that which you might call the New World, the New Earth, the transcended Earth. And they are the ones benevolent of heart that will be the ones who are like the ushers the ones who had such depth, such love, such forgiveness that they will usher in those who transcend and ascend into that world. They went first, for they were up to the task.

Many of the ones who left the Earth chose to leave so that they can populate the New Earth and begin to do the seeding of a new planet. There are animals, there are people, there are life forms on the new Earth that many say where are they where have they gone? And if you mourn the tragic lost there is no tragic lost. There has been suffering and what is lost, what is real, what always is and cannot be deathless nor birthless? Much of what you see around you is all illusion. Your body is not what you think it is. Nothing is as you think it is. And the new Earth is flourishing even when the tears are still being cried for those who left. Where did they go? They either went to the death kingdom or they went to the new Earth or they went back home to the place that they came from at a level of less suffering. No one is anywhere and spirit never dies.

So do not waste your time in one sense worrying about those who have come and those who have gone. Be in compassion, oh yes my brother. Care but see further, look deeper to where they went. You do not know where they went. Do not take my word for it, but the day will come when you shall see where they are, why they went, why they chose to reveal in equity, to be revealers of ignominy. Just as the new children chose to arrive and bring forth a new vibration into the essence of the planet. Many of those chose to leave the old vibration and enter the new vibration because there hearts were so pure and they chose that and they wanted an exit and they chose their form of exit. Why not leave and also, reveal the truth about what happens when consciousness is greedy and controlling and very low? So many things have played out upon the experiment of Earth and things are not always as they seem.

The importance is unconditional love, and unconditional compassion. And so it is important to care for every tree that was cut down and lost it's limbs. But where is that tree, where is that life, is it gone? Perhaps it is in a higher place, in a revered place. So I would say to you do not mourn, but do have compassion. I would say, in one sense, all death is tragic. Death will be transcended. It is not truth in the higher worlds. It is a necessity on a planet, such as Earth but all that is changing so welcome yourself to the shifting of the sands and to all the difficult stories, and these chapters are about to end.

Everything Is Changing

You say that you have trouble with your eyes? Your eyes are adjusting to vibrations, your eyes are changing the shape of the molecules within them. When we said that everything was changing in your world, all structures, all substance what did we mean? What were we talking about? We said that everything was changing. That means your physical body is going through massive changes and alterations. You are being redesigned from the inside out from the outside in. You are becoming a new species of light. How many times have we said that? And yet, how many of you still believe that something is wrong with you. Blurry vision, bad eyesight, pain here, pain there, spiritual fevers, and all the list of ramifications and all the list of symptoms, that the light workers, and even those that do not call themselves light workers are experiencing, is but a shift into higher frequency. It doesn't happen without changing something. Change is change and alteration is alteration and you are going up to a new frequency. It is also very intense and it may get even more intense.

Your inner sight is coming on line and your outer sight is going to change. Your eyes will change and your brain frequencies are changing and altering. No, it isn't about age. There are young children whose eyes are adjusting to four dimensional frequencies and higher. Sometimes it is hard to walk or to move. It could happen to a ten year old, or a fourteen year old, or the twenty four year old, or a forty four year old. The DNA is changing, you are changing at the level of the smallest bit of who you are, what we call sub-atomic, what we call the quark, what we call even smaller than the quark, the string. The very tiniest little string is being restrung, is being re-vibrated into a new frequency. Go and check your eyes out by an eye doctor then you will see. If the eye doctor can tell you that you are having problems with your eyes because of this or that, that they would know about then get eye glasses it is not the end of the world. If the eye doctor tell you that you should be seeing fine there is nothing wrong with your eyes then understand that what Djwhal has said is true. It could be either and it will be both. The changes are happening and yet there could be something wrong with your eyes, it happens. There is a weakness in the human body. It could happen but check it out

. Many people are going to the doctors because of this problem or that problem in the heart. Some of them have a disease frequency of disease others will find that there is no reason for it the doctors can find then the mind can rest. So check it out oh yes but let the mind rest. And in your case, if it is a problem with your eyes, it is also what Djwhal has just explained, because you are going up in frequency.

Closing

We have come to the end and it is time to close the session. You will get the information about St. Augustine and you will receive it within the space of your own channel which is by the way expanding and growing. So blessings to you, beloved one. We thank you for coming again to the court of love where we can exchange certain ideas and always exchange the love that is in my heart, and that is in your heart, that transcends physicality. So welcome to the wonderful intensity of the current ride into higher vibration. You are a major part of it, connected to All That Is. Blessings upon you in a shower of love and

I am Djwhal Khul again at your service with much love and much appreciation

A Personal Message From A friend

This was given to me from a good friend after I explained to her about a dream I had one night where I seemed to be going through all the seven levels of Initiation, all in one night. I know it was very symbolic representing an answer to my inner thoughts. Below is her assessment of my dream: I feel very strongly that it is beyond the number of an initiation, and anything we attach to the number, but that you are GROWING very big now and they want you to know that your upgrades are real, true, and that you are holding more light, that you are preparing at inner levels, for what is coming to you, which is the full revelation of who you are which must come from you, not me or anyone, and the preparations for what is going to be a lot of work when you shift to the New Earth. It is then that you will be doing a lot of what you want to do now, sort of, but the thing is all that you do until then, is all ONE thing. So you are moving fast now. You will be greeting and helping everyone adjust into the ONE Reality and the One Harmony that New Earth really is about. It is not going to be about divisions anymore. You will be major in that and work as a team with some others.

This just comes through. The initiation levels are metaphors, in a way, of your acceleration, your growth, your stepping forward, all the things you feel about yourself being confirmed, and given back to you in a way that has meant something to you, but it is not so much about actually passing initiations. Personally, I believe that you totally ARE in the 7th level now, anyway, so that may be part of it. But the important thing is that you are being supported by Spirit and told by Spirit that things are more EFFORTLESS with you, within you, even if the people all around you seem to still be struggling, so to speak. When you stop seeing things as struggles, the struggles start going away. Perception is a major key to the whole reality on Earth. Where your thoughts go, there you are. What you focus on, you bring to yourself. It is all true, so you are just in a really good space.

Chapter 18
Adama-High Priest of Telos under Mt. Shasta

Your Role As Romulus

Greetings beloved brother this is Adama. It is with joy and pleasure that we reconnect with you, as we are familiar with your focus on ancient Lemuria, as Romulus. As Romulus, you played an important role and you really were trying to teach the people of Lemuria in the capacity where you were standing in those days, about the right use of energy because the Mushaba Force that you are trying to bring back to the surface is nothing more than the primal energy. It is called by different names in different places and it is basically a feminine energy and is balanced with the polarity of the masculine in oneness. In the time of Lemuria this energy was very awesome until it got misused. As long as people used this energy with love, light and divine intention, it created magic and brought Lemuria to the height of glory, of perfection, that she had once attained. Eventually after many, many hundreds of thousands of years of evolution, a rift came in Lemuria and this wonderful energy started to be misused by some and eventually it become misused by more and more, until Lemuria felled in consciousness, and I am sure you are aware of that. You as Romulus did what you could to encourage people not to misuse this energy, but like many others you were not listened to. It is not that you failed, it is that in your intentions like so many others, you did what you could to prevent this.

Lemuria Fell In Consciousness

There were those that were faithful and those that failed and brought along with them the fall of Lemuria. It would never have happened, the misuse of this energy, if you could have had the masses join in the right use of it and stop those who were beginning to misuse this force. It is a little like that today, the light workers versus the masses. The light is now in a greater number than in the time of Lemuria during the fall. As a group of light workers today you are in sufficient numbers to reverse the tide and bring the masses back to the understanding of how to use this energy in a very wondrous way to create again Heaven on Earth. But the masses have free will and some will chose to leave the planet and some will chose to stay and change. In the time of Lemuria, it wasn't time for the ascension of this planet like it is now, so you are facing the fact that the ones that won't be a part of this will be leaving the planet. But those during the time of Lemuria who chose the left hand path and misused that wondrous energy did not leave the planet, this is why eventually the third dimensional aspect of Lemuria had to be destroyed. So here we are again today and you are all back on the surface as light workers trying to recreate what was lost in Lemuria, and you will recreate this in a much more wondrous way as a collective of light workers, as they all wake up. And what you are doing, is playing your role.

It is like a gigantic jigsaw puzzle and everyone is playing their piece of the puzzle. We are honoring you for what you are trying to do and for your wonderful book that you are publishing and We want to congratulate you for your book. It will help many, beloved one.

Questions

(Q). As Romulus, what was the movements that I taught in Lemuria?

(A). It was a movement of energy, first and foremost, and you were able to move your body, to move the energy in a particular fashion for a particular purpose of accomplishment, and this was only one of the ways. These are basically body movements that help move energy in the right direction. These movements are still being done today but not exactly with the intensity and focus of those times because the body mechanisms or actions and movements were very different during that time. It was used for healing and for creation. It was done along with the spoken word and your thoughts. You open the heart and that creates tremendous amounts of energy.

(Q). What do you know about Aleem and Paravun and our connection?

(A). Aleem and Paravun are young, and usually at that age, young people do not have the maturity but they have a certain maturity that is very exceptional. You can form a triangle with them in meditation and together you can be a powerful force. They definitely have a soul maturity and they are waking up at an earlier age than many young adults.

(Q). What was the Lemuria connection to the Black Race in Africa?

(A). Well, you have to realize that the continent of Mu was the motherland. It was a massive piece of land that was the continent of Mu, and there were temples all over the planet facing in the direction of Mu, in the ring and the circle. They were all strategically placed, looking at the motherland. Mu was the cradle of civilization which all civilizations extended from. It's not how Africa was connected to Mu, because everything was connected to Mu. The African people were a race of people that came from another planet. It was a different Creation and they were the Violet People. There were different kinds of people that came to populate the Earth and they came before the Fall in very, very much purity. The Black People that you have today were the Violet Race. They were violet and they were absolutely beautiful. Then there was the Crystal Race and many kinds of races and one was just as beautiful as the other.

(Q). When will humanity be allowed to visit the inner temple at Telos?

(A). Well, you can come to the inner temple anytime you want, in your etheric body. Any night you want to, before you go to sleep, ask to go there. In about maybe three or four years, humanity will be ready, at least some, to come physically to the inner temple. It will all depend on what happens to humanity as far as how quickly humanity will raise it's frequency so that it can come to the temple. The temple is a fifth dimensional temple and in humanity's present situation, body and frequency, it could not possibly come to the temple. Why? Because any unresolved issues that resonate with less than the Christ would be amplified thousands of times and they couldn't stand more than two seconds and they would have to get out. This amplification and all these energies have to be healed first and the physical body is not adapted to fifth dimensional frequency and it is working it's way up but it is not there yet. When can people come is when people can raise their frequency. In Telos we have many temples and they are all fifth dimensional and it would be impossible for anyone to come physically at this time.

Closing

So we have answered your questions my beloved brother. Well, it was my delight on behalf of the Lemurian Council and on behalf of Telos and it was our pleasure to connect with you today and I encourage you to continue in your search and in your work in spreading love around you. I am offering you the gift today of the heart because you are very much a heart person and we are offering you the gift that if you would like to connect with Adama, myself tonight in the temple, then come to the great Jade Temple and I will meet you there tonight in your Etheric body and we will do some heart openings for you. Make your intentions before you go to bed and I will send you our love and our gratitude for your light and for what you are doing. It is a temple of healing but it has many, many other things as well. Blessings beloved one!

Chapter 19
Ascended Master Afra Returns

Time Travel

This is Afra the Ascended Master and it's very interesting to look at the primal energy fields of the planet. So when you are wishing to study about the Mushaba Force you are also looking through time and also going back to an earlier time and one would have to say, that there is an aspect of time traveling in which one can go to the primal energy field of the Earth. What we see now manifested on the Earth is certainly a distortion of many different energies that have interacted and in some ways are becoming extremely destructive. Yet, if you were to go back in time, you could go back to where you are most comfortable, in the primordial Africa, where you would see the earlier tribes before they were corrupted by outsiders, you would see a particular unity, a particular primordial energy that was extremely harmonious and extremely in tune with the spirit world, extremely in tune with nature. Yes, you could say that it was naive yes, you could say that it was simplistic but it was also very primordial.

I want you to travel back in time with me to a time, perhaps in 1400 AD in this 2000 year period, I want you to go to a place that is called Swaziland which is now a country, where you have some deep roots, and place yourself in that context. I see there in this past life where you were a great dancer and I see you listening to the drums, I see you fire walking and you know what that is. I see you having many famous and powerful gifts of intense energy much like you are now, very intense. Because you understood even then that there was a manifestation of the Spirit, there were manifestations of the Mastery of Spirit that must be demonstrated on the Earth and you were living that reality.

So you can time travel back to that place and even further and even deeper before then, when the Earth was still forming, when the continents were still forming and when all energies were beginning to coalesce on the planet. So look at this force, the Mushaba Force as a connection with the Primordial Energy but look at it as a Primordial Energy that must be harnessed by the intention of the Mushaba Master. So you are, in a sense, like the magician on the tarot card who is bringing down light and directing it with intention. So you shall be reconnecting with your past life in Swaziland and the Primordial Energy of the Black People in the Continent of Africa. Great spiritual people, people of magnificent pride and connecting this to the sub- conscious of the earth. This is Afra good day and Mushaba Blessings!

Chapter 20
The reconnections bring forth a message

The Reconnections are the parts of ourselves, who had to un-connect with us in order for us to become human. They are now coming back to reconnect with everyone. These Beings, or this reconnection energy who any individual speaks with, are the parts of themselves that were disconnected. They come with a message that is related to you, as they know about you, since they are a part of your multi-dimensional being.

Simultaneous Parallel Existence

When you speak of this force you call Mushaba Force, there is a sense here of so many things. But among them is this linkage, this sense of gathering of ones alternative tools and equipment from within and from without. For within the physical world there is the reflection of what is within, do you understand this? So particularly, the emotion, the passion factor that has been so prominent in so many of your lifetimes and that is being so prominent in your lifetime now. We speak in the context of simultaneous parallel existence, as opposed to linear existence, as is outlined in what you know as reincarnation. Simultaneous parallel existence then is a gathering of these emotions within various contexts of reality and then brought through the pipeline and channeled specifically within a situation where there is need, interest and focus of concern and this lifetime where you chose to incarnate within the Black skin is very much connected with the physical element. This black element has enabled within it a closeness to the physical manifestation. Fine physical specimens who know instinctively to be grounded, how to relate to the Earth, not necessarily as the Earth but as a partner with it you see what we mean?

And so the tremendous emotional force and the force of the manifestation of magic that can then be channeled through a physical being, is what you're working on now. In perfecting your relationship to the physical, allowing that to spread out like a peacock's tail, you can then, at specific times and certain situations, take this tremendous force of manifestation this empathy, this Mushaba Force and use this ability to penetrate into the depths of the individuals with whom you are working. You will do it in such a way that you will not burn or injure them in anyway, as did those in the Atlantean environment, through the over usage of crystals. There was some abuse during that time and that is being perfected and corrected now, you see what I mean? The emphasis that we would bring to your already existing definition of Mushaba Force is the emphasis of profound and deep emotional linkage. The Mushaba Force, The Force Of Oneness will surround and protect you through the times of great change.

Manifesting That Which You Had The Most Trouble With

There are many that you will help worldwide but particularly those in the African decent. There is a sense of alienation in this society against self, against the very elements that are the strength of the African people, in favor of moving on into more westernized ideas. And those who hold on to the old traditional focuses, or maybe what you would call the core of African essence, are sometime pressured to give it up in favor of more forward thinking, modern concepts. There is a struggle in the whole world with this, with all people, and races but there is a need to integrate, and a desire to integrate, so that success and prosperity and functionality can happen in all the societies. Realize that those who manifest in a particular element or race, the black, the yellow, the red, the brown, the white etc., they are manifesting on a multi-dimensional level, in the area that they had the most trouble with. And so, the idea of the physical connection with the body, to use the body, to function in the body, to be comfortable as a body, then is the greatest challenge and also the greatest need and the message that, the Black race brings to the world.

An Arch Angelic Presence

There is an Arch Angelic base around you, particular the one that is known as Gabriel, sustaining, guiding and protecting and Gabriel is not a bad jazz player either! I want you to know, that all those who have been given the Oneness journey to share the concept, to process people upon their return to Oneness, have been usually severely cauterized in many areas. But as they open up, as they let loose of their pain, which is basically the resistance to these things, these things will remain there, but they will turn from battle scars to medals of honor.

Lion Head Figure

Now, concerning the lion head figure of the Sphinx, there is a very definite impression here of a kingship or one of your life experiences where you were a leader and a ruler. What is very definitely our energy on this, is that you are represented by the lion head figure. As we look into the face of the Sphinx, we see your face and that also brings to memory the idea of a kingship or rulership, not only in Egypt, but also in another land, which will be revealed specifically for some of that is withheld, until sequentially, it is time for you to begin to integrate that energy. But realize, that what comes forward for you now, is your realization of the many contexts in which you're a leader, and people come to you, and trust you, and follow you.

And then also you have to integrate the times in your leadership when there was a betrayal of trust, a particular failure of judgment that resulted in pain, death, and failure of a project. There is now within, you as you gather momentum once again for your leadership in the area of the Mushaba Force, hesitancy and doubt coming from these times, these periods where your judgment resulted in physical and emotional pain to other people. There is a sense of hesitancy of "will I make those same mistakes again?" Realize that, no, you will not and that now you will be guided by the pain of having experienced that. Because this neuro connection, that you carry within you, which is the Mushaba Force, is so powerful, you had to bring yourself a lot of grief in order to keep it from eating everybody up. Thank you and it was a pleasure speaking with you.

Chapter 21
A Closing Message

To all of you who have read this book, and have come to, in your own mind, some sort of conclusion and some sort of expanded awareness, know that the information provided has the intention of opening and expanding one's perception of truth and reality about humanity. We also want you to be fully aware of the lies and deceit perpetrated by those who wish to maintain control over humanity. The separation of the races has been a major piece of the control and domination of humanity on this Earth. We have to live and dream the dream that is said to be the impossible dream. What is this impossible dream? It is a dream which is
Possible, that people of all races are living together in a total oneness

To Dream And Impossible Dream

To dream an impossible dream, To reach the unreachable star, To live the true hearts desire, To be that which you came here to be, To move beyond separation and fear, To unite in the unity of love, To live in oneness among all humanity, To be what God intended us to be, To know ourselves in every aspect of being, To live the light that we are, To be free without attachments and judgments, Not to be separated by color and differences, To love unconditionally instead of hating one another, To forgive, release and let go, To embrace every part of who you are, To look at others and see yourself, To go within and find the answers to life questions. Is this truly an impossible dream? It is not! For this is where we are headed in a very quick fashion so, therefore, there is no impossible dream or unreachable star, for all things are possible. We have to stop putting limitations upon ourselves because of decisions made for us by others

Colorlessness

This book did not come from the root of color but from the foundation of colorlessness. This information is meant to uplift and inform. It all comes from a realm that has no color even though many things are referenced by color for the sake of human understanding. We are so trapped in this color of separation, not realizing that when we strip away the flesh, it is all the same, which is simply light! Simply Spirit! The idea is to bring forward the truth of all people who walked the Earth and did great works for humanity regardless of the color of skin they wore in that particular lifetime. For that same spirit would have worn a different color skin in another lifetime. We are attempting to bring forward the true history of humanity to Earth and we do not want you who read this book to think that it is about color, for it is not about color and never has been. It is all for lessons of true history and growth for all humanity. People are so quick to take information and run with it, with the intent to use it to either defend, or to attack and destroy, and to use it to put themselves up beyond someone else to feed the ego consciousness.

This information on the Black Race and Ascended Masters is intended to clear up some of the many distortion about the Black Race and the truth of what the original intent and purpose of the African people was and what they contributed to the evolution of Humanity. It is about knowing and acknowledging and about appreciation and gratitude for what a People has done to contribute their part to this whole divine plan for Earth's people. It is not to show up another race or to look better than another or point the finger and say "I told you so," because all that adds to separation and judgment instead of the healing and unity of humanity.

In The Final End Who Really Cares

In the final end to all this who really cares? What does it really matter who had what color skin, and did what, as long as the Divine plan is successful and humanity has accomplished it's purpose of Being because, all humanity will benefit, not just any particular race of people. So what if one people's piece was larger than another, or much smaller than another. It takes every piece to make the puzzle come together and the picture whole. So every piece is just as vital as the next. There is too much comparison as to who had the bigger piece of the puzzle. No one really did but God. God, the Creator, The Source, The Great Spirit or whatever handle you put on this Force of Creation is what had the biggest part of all of this.

When you cook a meal, aren't all the little things you do in preparation, just as important as cooking the meal? Aren't the little screws and bolts and nuts that hold a table together just as important as the table? What about the body? What about the little beat of the heart being as important as the big heart? You understand what I am saying. We should look at this before we start all the comparisons and separation with these little unimportant differences. Thank the Higher Wisdom that the body doesn't react this way or we would all be dead.

All Races Are Victims

So we hope that this book will prove to be of great value to all people of humanity and that the information brought forward is not misconstrued as something other than bringing truth and awareness to humanity, for reasons of growth and betterment for all people. Now I am not trying to sound like some simpleton person trying to talk that silly goody two shoes talk because I know the reality that we are faced with everyday. I am not under any illusions about what is going on and how people will react to this information. But yet we remain hopeful that much good will come from this and much healing between people and the races will begin to occur. The problem is, that we as a people, and I am not only speaking to the Black Race people, but all people, have been severely lied to by the few. We have all been taken for a ride on the good ship lollypop, while we suck on sweet lies and illusions. Because of where humanity is headed, the truth of Earth and its true history which is known from a higher perspective, must come forth. We cannot continue to live and sleep in darkness about what is. We cannot continue to ignore the fact that we have been manipulated and deceived about nearly everything we know and have been taught, since the manipulations came in and the many controlled the few. The White race is just as much a victim as the Black race or any other race, for that matter. The few are a class and race of their own that recognize no color, but only recognize their own inner circle of lineage and power. There is more to come as more and more of this truth is allowed to be accessed by the higher dimensional realms and record keepers who know and have the true history of Earth and it's inhabitants. Until then we thank you and greet you with the greetings of Divine Love and Oneness: Mushaba Blessings!

Appendix

Anakhanda Shaka Mushaba is available for worldwide travel to conduct workshops, lectures and the many services that he and his team of spiritual teachers have to offer. These services using the energy and frequency of the Mushaba Force, includes healings, soul clearings, energy field balance, cosmic egg realignment, opening portals for many purposes, and much more. These services can be done both in person and distance. For information on books, lectures, workshops and services please contact us at:

www.mushabaforce.com   E-mail: Mushaba1@yahoo.com
Mushaba Force-Mushaba Light-808-822-9390

Other upcoming and available books:

1. Mushaba Force – Mushaba Light

Original Prime Source

"The Primordial Energy of Creation"

2. You Can See-The Story of Maldion

Leader of the Good Darkness.

3. The Book of God and Goddess

4. Freedom and Empowerment- The Mushaba Race Project

Other Information

www.allowlove.com **The Trance Channel Team - 808-821-9606**

Rod and Katherine Russell is a trance channel team working together to serve the needs of humanity. Rod is a full trance channel and Katherine is an excellent conscious channel and gatekeeper. Their service is built on love and integrity. I highly recommend them for readings both group and private sessions. They have been excellent in assisting me in many ways through my walk. They also offer a variety of services from workshops, healings and more both in person and distance. For further information please visit their website.

Ascended Masters of Color - Ascended Beings of Light

Printed in the United States
64117LVS00001B/61